Shattered Window
Jordan Daniel Chitwood

"The King will reply, 'Truly I tell you, whatever you did for one of the least of these brothers and sisters of mine, you did for me (Matthew 25:40, NIV)."

SHATTERED WINDOWS & POINTLESS DREAMS

Jordan Daniel Chitwood

This book is dedicated to the least, the lost, the lonely,

and the forgotten.

Contents:

Foreword

Intelligent. Passionate. Honest. Real. Jordan's book or Jordan? Yes.

Jordan writes like he lives: With both deep conviction and daring love. That's not a popular combination these days. It's easy to find people whose unassailable convictions about all matters keep most of us at a respectful distance, observing their ways. Like watching lions at the zoo. Moreover, it's not a problem to find people who believe that real love never asks hard questions or makes people feel uncomfortable. It just makes people feel better. Like videos of baby animals. But Jordan's life is a refreshing reminder that the fruit of rooted convictions can be love. And that love, authentic love, can be grounded in firmly held convictions. Plus, the beauty of this book is that it's one that will actually be read. You know what I mean. We all have books we intend to read. Someday. I have shelves full of them. Long books with compelling covers and intriguing titles. And an inch of dust.

This book is divided into short, but far from shallow, chapters. The kind of chapters that invite us to think, to wrestle, to possibly even make more informed and better decisions. All before we finish our lattes. Bottom line: This book is filled with real life examples. So, if you're into real life, then you'll appreciate the authenticity of the writing. Much of it is also told in stories: Engaging, memorable stories drawn from Jordan's own joys and struggles, and from his perceptive observations about life and faith, loss and suffering. And hope. Real hope—the kind that's discovered in the midst of disappointment and doubt. Even death. That's probably what makes *Shattered Windows & Pointless Dreams* so compelling: It's meant to be read with the broken glass still on the floor and the dreams of yesterday drifting out into the night. But waiting for the morning.

-Todd Faulkner

Disclaimer: I Believed

"You never know how much you really believe anything until its truth or falsehood becomes a matter of life and death to you." - *C.S. Lewis*

"Jordan, do you understand why you are here?" The principal asked me after I had taken a seat in his office. I honestly had no idea why I had been called down to sit in the room of despair. I was typically a respectful kid in high school and rarely did things that resulted in discipline. I shook my head no and stayed silent.

"Jordan, we have been receiving reports from different students claiming you are sending them and their family members to hell. Is this true?"

Once again, I was silent. I could not recall sending anybody to hell, but I had been going from lunch table to lunch table evangelizing. My church youth group had recently gotten back from a youth conference and I was on fire for God. I thought this was what people did when they were experiencing a spiritual high. After shaking my head no once again, my principal replied:

"Well, Jordan, we have a report here that says you have been going around to different lunch tables and asking others what their beliefs are. This one, in particular, says a girl shared her story with you about how her mom died by suicide. During the story, the girl says she told you she ended up going to church to seek hope. She was wondering if her mom could possibly still be in Heaven, but the church pastor told her because her mom died by suicide, she was condemned to hell. The report further explains that instead of comforting the girl, you took it upon yourself to confirm what the pastor said. That is why you are here today."

I was shaking. Sweat began to form at my brow and my fists clenched up tighter than a double-knotted shoelace. I believed if somebody died by suicide, it showed they did not have a relationship with God, which meant their fate was pretty straightforward. So, I got defensive...

"Why is it wrong for me to share my beliefs with her? I am a Christian, after all. I'm not supposed to stay silent about these things."

"Jordan, I am a Christian too. And whether or not what the pastor said or what you said is true, the way you responded towards her grief is not what Christ would have done. She was seeking comfort and encouragement, and instead, she is now more shattered than before. It is not wrong for us to share our heart with someone, but only if we do so in a pure way, with a pure heart, at the correct time. Even if we say something that happens to be true, we must navigate those conversations with grace. Do you understand what I am saying to you?"

I wish I had. I wish at the time I fully understood what he was telling me to do—but I didn't. I didn't understand why it was so damaging to share what I believed with everyone. I nodded my head yes anyways, grabbed my coat, and left.

I wish I believed then what I believe now.

I believed that if you were a Christian, you had to be a Republican. I grew up in Indiana—an extremely conservative state—where everyone and their mother was a Republican. There is nothing wrong with being a Republican, but because my family and almost everyone I knew associated with the Republican Party, I never saw a fair representation of other ways to view the world.

I believed that homosexuality was a one-way ticket to hell. Anyone who was part of the LGBTQ+ community was living in sin because they were pursuing relationships with members of the same sex. If they truly loved God, God would take away their temptation and would make them straight. All they needed to do was "pray the gay away." Regardless of how many conversations I had with people who held opposing beliefs, I was very firm in believing gay people went to hell.

I believed racism was dead and gone. How could we still be living with a mindset that was supposed to have died in the 1960s? I believed that an "America First" model was the best. America is God's country... right? I believed that the entire Bible was written perfectly, and therefore, the interpretations were straightforward. I believed that someone could be 100 percent correct in his or her beliefs. I believed that if you prayed hard enough, your mental illness would go away. I believed that the Church would never betray you. I believed that a prayer was what secured salvation.

I believed these things... and they affected the way I treated and viewed everyone.

If you believed these things, or still believe these things, then this book is for you. Do not throw this aside just yet. I challenge you to read this book with an open mind and a heart willing to listen. I encourage you to dive in with a passion for dialogue. I ask that you approach this book with the understanding that we live in a world with *Shattered Windows &*

Pointless Dreams—a world so far from how Jesus wants us to live and in desperate need of reconciliation. A world broken because of sin, suffering, and selfishness, and dreams deemed pointless because of generational poverty and generational abuse. A world where windows are shattered and there is no protection from evil in the lives of our neighbors. A world that encourages individuals to live with a "me first" attitude. A world filled with grief and suffering. A world divided by political parties, geography, religious affiliations, sexual orientations, Scriptural interpretations, genders, tragedies, races, ethnicities, social barriers, school systems, money, and fame.

We live in a world in which the Church has strayed so far from how Jesus designed it that it has become normal to condemn specific lifestyles. Our reasoning? Other ways of living aren't like ours. We live in a world where Christians ignore half of the Bible because the other *stuff* threatens to make us uncomfortable… you know… *like Jesus*.

Communities are generations deep in poverty and have few chances, if any, to break out of the cycle. Kids are growing up without their parents because their mom and dad didn't want them or couldn't support them. Girls and boys are sold into sex trafficking and have to live with the scars of abuse for the rest of their lives. Gun violence is taking innocent lives every year. Our world is consumed by capitalism, making successful dreams obtainable only to the privileged. How did we get here?

Questions on Top of Questions

Some of the greatest books I have ever read were about topics I was terrified to approach. Some of the most life-changing authors with whom I engaged were individuals I believed were going to hell. As you read this book, I challenge you to keep an open mind but a ready mind—a mind willing to hear new ideas but also prepared to study them and wrestle with them yourself. This book will stretch you, but I pray that it stretches you closer to God. This book will challenge you to view how you treat others who are different than you. This book will encourage you to look past yourself and pursue others the way Jesus did. My hope for my readers is that this book will continually assist you in wrestling with topics that are not easily settled or put to bed.

As I have grown in my faith, I have found myself questioning everything I believed: The books that seemed concrete, the verses that were memorized, the parables that were taught, the firm stances on suicide, politics, homosexuality, religion, and God.

Everything. Questioned.

Because of this, I also ask that you wrestle with the questions and themes presented in this book. Don't simply take my word for it—study them yourself. Challenge the material and come to grips with what you believe. I have wrestled with material that many Christians would deem heretical or "off-limits." I have studied and prayed about things that many would shy away from because of what *they* believed. I believe the greatest growth comes in times we are the most uncomfortable. Why should I limit myself to things that are comfortable when the very things that make me uncomfortable could be true?

It was throughout this process of faith cleansing that the suffering of the world became personal to me. Not long ago, a friend of mine had a rock thrown through her family's window because her family chose to take someone from their hometown to court to protect her sisters. That act of violence rattled everyone in the house. It's intimidating, it's shocking, it's hateful, and it happened where one is supposed to feel comfortable and safe. It dissolves the illusion of comfort and safety. Windows are not just shattered and dreams are not merely pointless, they are shattered and made pointless at the hands of sin and hate that come crashing in.

We live in a world where windows are shattered and dreams are deemed pointless every day.

Where is the beauty in this, God?

Is there hope?

Is there justice?

Does this include me?

What about the children who were born in a developing country? Is there hope for them? What about the daughter who was abused by her alcoholic mother? Is there hope for her? What about those being bullied because they are interested in different things than us? Is there hope for them? What about the victims of human trafficking? Is there hope for them? The International Labour Organization estimates that there are 20.9 million victims of human trafficking globally. Sixty-eight percent of them are trapped in forced labor. Twenty-six percent of them are children.

Is there hope for them?

What role should the Church play in the lives of those with *Shattered Windows & Pointless Dreams*?

It's All About Me

For too long, many of us have lived comfortably. For too long, Christians who claim to follow Jesus have lived in a way that is opposed to what He wants from us. For too long, many of us have put our needs above others' and have shoved everyone else behind us.

I am living proof of this. I waited on the sideline for someone else to take the lead. I remember being overwhelmed by fear. I allowed the pain of others to go unnoticed. I refused to recognize my privilege and placed others in the back of my mind. I used excuses such as:

My pain is more important.

My safety is more important.

My family is more important.

My career is more important.

My reputation is more important.

My country is more important.

My lifestyle is more important.

My comfort is more important.

My story is more important.

After realizing I was using these excuses, I felt convicted to change. This is when I became a firm believer that we are called to do two things while we are here on earth.

1. Love God

2. Love Others

I believe everything worth doing falls under those two areas. Nothing else matters if those two commands are jeopardized. Does this mean we *have* to pursue others if we claim the name of Christ? Absolutely. In Matthew's testimonial account of Jesus found in his Gospel, Jesus was approached with the same question:

"Hearing that Jesus had silenced the Sadducees, the Pharisees got together. One of them, an expert in the law,

*tested him with this question: "Teacher, which is the
greatest commandment in the Law?" Jesus replied:
"'Love the Lord your God with all your heart and with
all your soul and with all your mind.' This is the first and
greatest commandment. And the second is like it: 'Love
your neighbor as yourself.' All the Law and the Prophets
hang on these two commandments (Matthew 22:34-40,
NIV)."*

John simplifies this command in his testimonial account
of Jesus. John writes in his Gospel,

*"A new command I give you: Love one another. As I
have loved you, so you must love one another. By this
everyone will know that you are my disciples, if you love
one another." (John 13:34-35, NIV)*

People are watching and waiting for the Church to be
the Church that revolutionized the world two thousand years
ago. We often believe we have to argue and prove that God
exists. I don't think that is the case. In my experience, my
actions of love, grace, and truth have done more for the

Kingdom of God than the debates about Scripture I have had. Don't get me wrong, the Bible is an incredibly powerful source that points us to the life of Jesus; but much like the trap that the Pharisees fell into, we can have all the Biblical knowledge that is possible and still miss the point of Jesus. My mother said it best: "It is important to not just rely on our head knowledge of God, but also our heart knowledge of God." The way we love and pursue those with *Shattered Windows & Pointless Dreams* shows how much we are willing to love and pursue Christ.

Answer the Call

Their pain matters. Their needs matter. Their dreams matter. Their families matter. Their lives matter. *Shattered Windows & Pointless Dreams* is a call to action. It is a call for those who claim the name of Christ to adhere to a sacrificial lifestyle: A lifestyle that pursues the least of these. A lifestyle that says their lives are more important than mine. A lifestyle that reflects the walk of Jesus. There are gifted people in this world that have the potential to move mountains but lack the resources to do it. Our neighbors need help. Jesus loved those who were thrown away, empowered the marginalized, and saved those who needed healing. Jesus risked His safety, His family, His finances, His comfortable lifestyle, His friends, His reputation, and His life to love everyone.

As we study different testimonial accounts from the Bible throughout this book, we will see that it is our obligation to do the same. Throughout the Gospels, the topic that Jesus proclaimed the most was the Kingdom of God. For Him, this Kingdom is ushered in through the law of love. To live in the Kingdom is to pursue and love others in radical ways that most of the world does not understand.

With that being said, the point of *Shattered Windows & Pointless Dreams* is not to completely change your views on what you believe. My desire for this book is to connect the things you believe to the way Jesus lived. If the things you believe prevent you from loving others because of their lifestyle, then that is something I pray changes. I beg you to ask yourself these questions:

1. What is stopping me from loving others?
2. Do we believe God only pursues us, in America?
3. Are we willing to live like Jesus?

At the end of the day, if you finish this book and are at a point of discouragement, I pray that this question comes to your mind: Am I closer to loving God and loving others the way Jesus did? I pray the conclusion you come to is "YES!" I hope your faith is strengthened by reading this book, not damaged. I pray that you address your own situation, in your context, and figure out what it looks like to get messy for YOU. It is going to look different for everyone. Some of the things I suggest may not be relevant for you—do not use that as a cop-out to ignore the context you have been placed in. I encourage you to use it as an excuse to venture into your community—willing to be there for anyone in any way that God has asked you to be—even if it is different than what I suggest.

I invite you on this journey with me as we explore together a world filled with *Shattered Windows & Pointless Dreams*.

Chapter 1: Let's Get Messy

"The world is noisy and messy. You need to deal

with the noise and uncertainty." - Daphne Koller

I remember sitting in Dr. Majeski's Christian Ministry class my sophomore year of college at Anderson University, absolutely devastated by what I was hearing. She said, "The world will tell you to be comfortable. The world will tell you to live with a Western mindset—a mindset that encourages stability, safety, pleasure, and wealth. A lifestyle that will tell you to put your needs first. That is not the Jesus model. Jesus. Got. Messy."

Jesus.

Got.

Messy.

Those words shattered my view of following Jesus. I began processing these statements over and over again in my head and attempted to make sense of the spiritual implications that this claim entailed. Questions were bombarding my brain from every direction. I wondered:

What does it mean to get messy?

How do I risk my safety and still stay... safe?

What if I am not called to serve... them?

In the middle of the chaos, I felt something tug on my heart. It felt as though a gust of wind was pulling me forward. Something was calling me to lean in and place aside my biases. In the middle of this class session, I knew I was being challenged to get messy, and I wasn't sure if I liked it. I didn't even know where to begin. *This theology terrified me.*

Have you had a similar experience that left you gasping for air as you attempted to breathe underwater in the midst of new material? While my experience may not seem as faith-threatening as yours, Dr. Majeski's words challenged my entire belief system. She was encouraging me to get messy in a world with *Shattered Windows & Pointless Dreams*—something I was attempting to do already within my own boundaries, but not the boundless love of God. Up until that point, I thought I did a decent job with the "loving God" part of Matthew 22 but had not fully understood what it looked like to love others. What was foreign to me, and might be foreign to you as well, was that loving God and loving others cannot be separated. In order to truly *love God*, we must also *love others*.

And that means getting messy.

The Church is Afraid to Get Messy

I began studying how Christians, including myself, loved others who were described as *"messy."* Individuals or groups of people who don't believe, act, live, or look like we do. My findings were discouraging. I realized that Christianity has become an exclusive faith system with more *rules* and *expectations* than *grace* and *truth*. Many would argue that because we are Christians, we are *clean people,* and other religions, beliefs, lifestyles, or socioeconomic statuses are *messy* because of the way they live and the things they believe. By living with this mindset, we encourage individuals to come as they are unless they are messy. We want individuals to fit into *our* criteria. Criteria such as:

Dress a certain way on Sundays.

Worship a specific way during service.

Take good notes during the sermon.

Sit towards the front in order to experience the Holy Spirit.

Tithe in order to be a member of the church.

Only men can preach from the pulpit.

Leave your addictions and temptations at the door in order to come in.

And then we have criteria that need to be met in order to affirm that others have a relationship with God. Criteria such as:

You must go to church on Sundays if you are a follower of Christ.

You need to be a Republican in order to be a Christian.

You need to be a Democrat in order to be a Christian.

You need to be baptized in order to receive salvation.

You need to be invested in the church first and the community second.

You need to read the Bible every day.

And then we take it so far as to say that we get to decide whose heart is pure and which souls receive salvation. We teach things such as:

> If you say a prayer, you will receive the ticket to salvation.

> If you have *that* lifestyle, you clearly cannot have a relationship with God.

> Your depression can be prayed away; seek God and He will give you rest.

> Your addiction can be stripped from you; all you need is to ask God and you shall receive.

> Your lustful desires will be eliminated if you read the Bible every day.

> If you don't agree with me, you are wrong.

> If you have suicidal thoughts, you aren't relying on God.

> If you struggle with temptation, you aren't serving your community enough.

And then there are even churches that will condemn people to hell for questioning their criteria. If this has been your story, I sincerely apologize.

When Dr. Majeski encouraged me to get messy, everything I had learned was being questioned. All of the things I believed were fair game to be challenged. I needed to place my expectations of the Church aside in order to dive into what God was preparing for me. After witnessing firsthand how I, along with my brothers and sisters in Christ, treated those who believe or live differently than us, I knew it was time for me to seek humility. Paul says it best in his letter written to the church in Corinth:

> *"For the foolishness of God is wiser than human wisdom,*
> *and the weakness of God is stronger than human strength*
> *(1 Corinthians 1:25, NIV)."*

This verse challenges my arrogance by claiming even God's *foolishness* and *weaknesses* are still *wiser* and *stronger* than me on my best day. This entire idea of getting messy means we have to be willing to step forward, outside of our comfort zone, in order to love God and love others the way Jesus did. Getting messy means we have to be willing to pursue people with *Shattered Windows & Pointless Dreams*. Getting messy means we must seek humility in everything we do and pursue others with grace. Sometimes that means saying yes to things we aren't sure about, and other times it means saying no to things we were confident in.

Throughout this journey, these are a few of the questions I wrestled with. You may have these questions as well: What does it look like for me to live like Jesus? What does it mean to enter into a narrative that places others' needs above my own? What does it look like to truly love God and love others the way Jesus did? Am I wrong for believing what I do? These are some questions we will be wrestling with for the entirety of the book.

I want you to understand that getting messy isn't easy and it looks different for every person. As I cleaned out my spiritual closet, I found out more about myself than I care to admit. God began chipping away pieces of my heart that were hardened due to years of abused theology and challenged me to start doing life with people society deemed messy.

Where to Begin on this Messy Journey

Searching through the Gospels, I recognized that Jesus sat and ate with messy people of His day all the time. In His time period, religious leaders didn't like the idea of their Messiah hanging out with tax collectors, prostitutes, castaways, lepers, the marginalized, and everyone in between. In fact, they hated that idea so much, they killed Him for it. And yet, Jesus spent His entire ministry inviting messy people to share a meal with Him that were labeled as "messy."

Now, it is our turn.

Table fellowship is a concept that Jesus used over and over during His time on earth. In His culture, table fellowship was as simple as sharing a meal with those who shared your beliefs. Jews ate at the same table as individuals with similar societal rank, lifestyles, and beliefs as them. This is why those deemed "unclean" or "sinful" were not welcomed at tables with religious Pharisees or political leaders (see Galatians 2:11-14). If you were a Jew, you ate with Jews. If you were a leper, you ate with lepers. If you were an adulterous woman, then you would hide in shame until it was safe for you to go out. When Jesus entered the picture, He changed all of that. Jesus ignored what culture encouraged Him to do and invited *everyone* to the table.

Table fellowship is now an authentic and raw experience that welcomes everyone to share a meal.

I learned that If I wanted to understand what it meant to get messy, I must first be willing to eat with people whom society described as messy. This was a bitter pill for me to swallow. However, Jesus spent countless hours sharing a meal with everyone regardless of their brokenness. In the Gospel of Luke alone there are ten unique cases in which Jesus shares a meal with different groups of people. You can find these examples here:

1. 5:27-32. Jesus shares a meal at Levi's house with tax collectors and sinners.
2. 7:36-50. Jesus shares a meal at Simon's house with Pharisees, guests, and women.
3. 9:10-17. Jesus feeds over 5,000 people (only men were counted).
4. 10:38-42. Jesus has a meal with Mary and Martha.
5. 11:37-52. Jesus has a meal at a Pharisee's house.
6. 14:1-24. Jesus has a meal at a Pharisee's house with Pharisees and other guests.
7. 19:1-10. Jesus shares a meal at Zacchaeus' house.
8. 22:14-38. Jesus shares a meal with his disciples—including the one who would betray Him (Judas), the one who would deny knowing Him (Peter), and the one who would lose faith after His death (Thomas).

9. 24:28-32. Jesus shares a meal with individuals on the road to Emmaus.

10. 24:36-43. Jesus shares a meal with His disciples after the resurrection.

While these examples are only from Luke, the rest of the Bible contains many more. For us, sharing a meal seems like common courtesy. We might glance over those verses and quickly move on to the more interesting parts of Scripture. However, Jesus didn't glance over people as if they were a number, He welcomed every single person to share a meal with Him.

Every. Person. Welcomed.

Walk the Talk

At its core, table fellowship is about a person's willingness to get messy. While eating food is always enjoyable (for many of us, too enjoyable), it is not the reason Jesus welcomed everyone to the table. Jesus invited people of different backgrounds, lifestyles, and sins to His table because He was not ashamed to be seen with individuals society despised. Jesus understood that if He was going to *share* with the world the power and love of

God, He needed to *show* the world the power and love of God. Inviting someone different than us or even someone we struggle to love may seem difficult enough, but Jesus went as far as to eat with His enemies. Table fellowship challenges us to place our egos aside and focus on humbly seeking God's will. How far are we willing to go to love others?

Dr. Majeski revolutionized the way I viewed being a follower of God. However, she was not all talk—she was living proof of *walking the talk*. While working full-time as a professor at Anderson University, Dr. Majeski felt the call to pursue and serve women in the sex trade. In 2010, she, along with a few close friends, felt the urge to help women step out of fear and walk in love. Dr. Majeski teaches classes at the university during the day and then visits local strip clubs and shares a meal with women who are working there in the evenings. Without an agenda, Dr. Majeski began building relationships with women whose lives were shattered and whose dreams seemed pointless. She began investing her time and energy into creating a safe environment for them to vent and share their stories. After a few years, Dr. Majeski became the CEO and founder of an organization called Stripped Love. Their mission challenges individuals to start walking with others: "Stripped Love exists to continue empowering women to step out of fear and into love." I had the privilege of partnering with Stripped Love for a few in-house events they held; such as a Christmas party and an Easter egg hunt for the women and their children. It was incredible to see Dr. Majeski pursue everyone, regardless of their lifestyle or their baggage. Dr. Majeski to this day is still getting messy, just like Jesus.

So invite someone over for dinner. Ask someone messy to have lunch. Spend an hour with someone you normally wouldn't. Have coffee or go see a movie with a person who drives you crazy. Embrace the mess of everyone around you and recognize that there is more going on than sharing a meal. Jesus chose table fellowship because of what it meant to share a meal in His culture with others. What does that look like for us in our context? What does it look like to "share a meal" with someone different than us? What does it mean to get messy in our lives with others?

Challenge yourself by creating an environment that welcomes all to your table regardless of their beliefs, lifestyles, cleanliness, or baggage.

Chapter 2: Does THIS Include THEM?

"Some people come into our life as a blessing, while others come into our life as a lesson, so love them for who they are instead of judging them for who they are not." - *Yolanda Hadid*

Yes.

Them.

That person who crossed your mind in the previous chapter. That family member with different views than you, maybe politically, religiously, or philosophically — it definitely includes them. Actually, the people we consider "*them*" as opposed to "*us*" are the exact individuals Christ calls us to love and pursue. The reality is, a lot of us live too comfortably. Those we want to pursue are *too* different from us. Individuals who tug at our hearts are *too* messy. However, it is our neighbors whom we paint as *untouchables* that Christ paints as *desirable*.

Not too long ago I was having a conversation with my brother-in-law about why our generation (millennials) are leaving and refusing to go to church. For years this has been the question Church leaders have wrestled with and discussed.

However, for millennials, it is a pretty simple answer: Millennials are tired of witnessing churches and Christians abuse the Word of God and ignore the command from God to love and pursue everyone equally (see John 13:34-35). Society labels millennials as watered-down Christians who are "too accepting" and "unequipped to preach the Gospel." In fact, it's not just millennials. Older Christians who are pursuing individuals with *Shattered Windows & Pointless Dreams* may also find themselves labeled the same way. The reality is, it takes more compassion, courage, discernment, and love to preach the Gospel through our actions than it does through quoting Scripture. Perhaps from a different perspective, millennials aren't causing the death of the Church; maybe we are requiring that the Church finally rise and live the way Jesus did.

Eliminate *"Them"* Terminology

It is impossible to love shattered people the way Jesus did when we have an agenda. Sometimes that agenda is an "America First" model. Sometimes that agenda means bringing people to a place where we are comfortable, rather than pursuing them where they are. Sometimes that agenda means giving up on people because they do not believe what we do.

It is saddening to realize that Jesus and His family would not receive access to America today because they would be considered "them." Matthew writes in his testimonial account of Jesus that when Jesus was a baby, He and His parents, Joseph and Mary, had to flee their home and escape to Egypt. They were refugees seeking asylum in order to avoid death (see Matthew 2:1-15). It makes me wonder if Jesus, Joseph, and Mary would be turned away from our borders because they would be considered illegal immigrants. I do not want to meet Jesus one day and have to apologize for turning Him away because of fear. Now, you might be confident that you would not turn Jesus away today, but Jesus declared that whatever we do for our neighbors, we do for Him (see Matthew 25:40).

Friends, we are Christ's followers *first*. Above everything else, our mission to invite everyone to the table should never change. This does not mean we cannot be honest with those with whom we disagree, but it does mean we must build a relationship *first*.

For Christ, there is never *them,* there is only *us.* We are all sinners. We are all different. We are all living life trying to figure out how to move forward. Not everyone has the same god as me. Not everyone has the same political party as me. Not everyone raises their kids the same way. Not everyone has the same sexual orientation. Not everyone has the same experiences. Christ loves us anyway. We've got to stop being a Church that lives for the "good ol' days." The beauty of the Bible is that it is an ongoing narrative. Because of this, the way we pursue others is always going to be changing. We cannot keep looking back when the world we are trying to reach is moving forward. While tradition itself can be a great thing, it needs to be continually evaluated and remain fluid with each generation. For example, for the longest time, the Church strictly sang hymns during worship. Individuals connected with the powerful words and triumphant sound of the organ playing. While hymns are still powerful, the style of music that the next generations are connecting with is much different. If the Church wants to reach the next generation through music, we need to evaluate the type of music that we are playing for worship.

Because of this, I challenge us to completely get rid of

the mindset, "I am correct and everyone who disagrees with me must be wrong." Telling everyone why they are wrong while believing we are absolutely correct moves us backward.

I had a friend in class once say, "Okay, I get that we are supposed to love everyone and form relationships with people we disagree with religiously... but when do we get to tell them that they are wrong?" I sat there shocked that those words had left his lips. Is that how we want to be known? As Christ-followers who tell others they are wrong? Is that what we are called to do? There is a time and a place to have every possible conversation we can think of, but we are not commanded to blatantly tell people they are wrong. Only after we have formed a relationship with others built on the foundation of love and trust do we have permission to share our heart. An effective way to share our heart is by asking questions that invite conversation. Boldly telling individuals they are wrong does not invite conversation.

We often believe that others won't know our stance or the Church's stance on an issue if we aren't vocal and firm about what we believe. Take homosexuality, for example. Many individuals who believe homosexuality is a sin have a hard time being friends with someone who is gay. Their fear stems from the idea that if we show love to gay people in any way, then they will think we agree with their choices. I will share more about this in chapter three, but I will say this: I personally have never met a gay person who did not already know how many Christians feel about the LGBTQ+ community. The real issue is that I have also never met a gay person who felt genuinely loved by the Church. You may have heard it said before, but we are becoming a community of believers more commonly known for what we are against, rather than whom we love. If we truly love God, we are called to love "them."

Through it all, rely on God to provide you with guidance on how to handle every situation. Sometimes it will mean having a conversation, sometimes it will not. When we skip chapters in order to get to the end of the book quicker, the result can be damaging.

Love Is

Love is a process. Love is a relationship. Love is a choice. Love is a journey that invites those we consider "*them*," those with *Shattered Windows & Pointless Dreams,* to our table. Love reaches out and embraces the least of these. Love challenges us to pursue our neighbors regardless of their situation. That is love. That is what love requires of me. That is what love requires of you. There is no "them" in the Kingdom of Heaven—only "us."

So, who is "*them*" to you? Whom do you struggle to love? When Jesus calls us to love our neighbor, who is your neighbor? Let me share a few stories that will paint a picture of the neighbors and the "them" God graciously placed in my life to love.

Is This for Carryout or Delivery?

As soon as I turned sixteen I started applying for jobs. I was motivated and determined to start making money so I could enjoy doing things normal teenagers do—you know, like buying Big Macs and going to late-night movies. Because I was in high school and needed flexible hours, I applied at Pizza Hut, Subway, and Office Depot. After numerous calls and interviews, I was offered a kitchen position making pizzas at Pizza Hut. I actually called them five times (once every five days), asking if they had time to review my application, until they brought me in for an interview. Whether I was qualified for the position or just annoyed them is up for debate.

About two years in, a new manager approached me with this question:

"Jordan, are you a Christian?"

The question took me by surprise. Typically on your first day, you don't go around asking people what their beliefs are. Even in the food industry, which has its fair share of odd workers, a more appropriate conversation starter might include the weather or the Pacers game the night before. For a brief second, a wave of anxiety covered my body. I loved my job at Pizza Hut and did not want to ruin any relationships with my co-workers because I believed in God. However, I took a risk anyway and responded honestly.

"Yes, I am. Why?"

He said, "That's what I thought. I checked all of the employees' Facebook profiles this weekend and yours looked very spiritual. I just want to tell you this right away: I don't care what you believe, but don't force me to believe it. I do not believe it and I do not want to believe it. Keep your God out of our relationship."

While it may seem odd, this response was an "exhale moment" for me. I was relieved. He did not care what I believed, and frankly, I did not care what he believed either. All he was interested in was whether or not I had a good work ethic and could make pizzas on time. I went home that night after my shift and tried to forget the conversation, but something was tugging on my heart. I immediately began trying to figure out how I could be a light for the Gospel when I was silenced in doing so. There was something about this manager that seemed off and I desperately wanted to find out more. I started processing questions such as:

Why is he so against God?

What happened in the midst of his story that he came to this conclusion?

What can I do to show him who God is without pushing him further away?

Connor and I started to form a relationship over the course of a few months. He was a hard worker with a sense of humor that never ceased to amaze me. I realized he deeply cared about people and wanted his business to thrive. Day after day Connor would show up early for his shift and leave late, making sure his team was fully taken care of and his customers were happy. At the most random times, he would share a bit more of his story with me. We started to become closer and our relationship continued to grow. I stayed silent about God but was there for him. Throughout everything he was sharing with me, I came to the realization that ***all he really needed was a friend***— one without an agenda. He needed someone he could trust at a time when he was consumed by darkness.

Connor started sharing with me how he was a recovering alcoholic. For years, Connor masked the presence of his pain with the presence of a bottle. He had two kids and a wife that he adored, but I could tell there was something painful he was covering up. There was something beneath the outer layer he refused to let me see. This made me want to share the hope and light I find in Jesus with him so much more—but God insisted I stay silent.

After three years of working at Pizza Hut, it was time for me to move on. College was calling my name and I was ready for a new adventure. I said my goodbyes and promised to keep in touch with everyone and then walked out the door feeling defeated. An entire year I had prayed, walked with, laughed with, and been a friend to Connor. God reminded me that I was not simply being his friend so he could find Jesus. I was being his friend because he needed one more than ever.

Connor and I stayed in contact with each other after I left for college. Every once in a while we would text each other memes and random jokes and ask how each other's families were doing. Roughly two years later I saw "God's Not Dead 2" in theaters. If you have seen the film, then you may be rolling your eyes because you know where I am going with this. At the end of the movie, the Newsboys encourage viewers to pull out their phones and text everyone in their contacts that God is NOT dead. I decided to take a risk and finally send Connor a text message about the hope I find in Jesus. The text went something like this:

"Connor, I care a lot about you. You mean a lot to me and I see that you are hurting. I know you told me never to bring up God around you, but I don't want to live my entire life wishing that I had. I want you to experience the joy of Christ that I have in my life. I love you man, and miss you."

His response?

"Thanks, Jordan, for reaching out. But I find my joy elsewhere."

SERIOUSLY GOD!? I waited for three years to have that

conversation. I was patient and spent hours building a relationship with him and that was his response? You mean to tell me that texting my entire contact list because a movie told me to doesn't always work? I set my phone down, talked with my wife, and headed home. I remember telling God, "I have literally done everything I can with him. If You are going to step into his life it is going to have to be through someone else. I pray that someone else can influence him. He is experiencing pain from his past and I pray that someone can help him find healing." I finally gave up control of the situation. I was doing my best to be his friend without an agenda. God was continuously reminding me to love him and be Connor's friend regardless of the god he followed. Even if he never came to Christ, God had him in the palm of His hand.

Roughly a year later, I saw Connor post on Facebook that he was looking to have dinner with someone. Since I lived in Anderson and he lived in Fort Wayne, I jokingly posted a comment that if he wanted to drive to Anderson I would love to host him for dinner. His response?

"Call me."

I picked up the phone, dialed his number, and was greeted

by a man in tears. In between breaths, he told me that he was completely broken. Connor had lost his job at Pizza Hut, been fired from his next job due to drinking, was struggling with his alcohol addiction now more than ever, and had been kicked out of the house by his wife. He had to report to court because of a DUI and did not know where else to turn. His life was completely shattered and he had no idea where to go.

He needed a friend.

I got in my car and drove an hour to meet him halfway at McDonald's. He unpacked everything he had experienced in the last year—including all of the pain he was going through in the past few weeks. I sat there speechless. How do I respond to someone who is shattered without sharing about the hope I personally find in God? All I wanted to do was uplift him and help him find true joy, but something told me this was not the time. *He did not need to hear about the life he could have; he needed someone to listen as he talked about the life that he did have.* At the very end of the conversation I asked him this:

"Connor, why me? Why now?"

He responded, "Jordan, there is something special about you. I know I can always count on you to be there for me. There are not many friends in my life I can say that about."

His response filled me with joy. This was what God needed me here for. I truly believe this is why I worked at Pizza Hut. Connor needed a friend. He needed someone he could trust with his mess. I had not successfully shared the Gospel with him like I personally wanted, but I had shown him what it meant to love your neighbor through our relationship, and that was sharing the Gospel as Jesus did.

We parted ways and I didn't hear from him for a year. I tried calling him and texting him but he never responded. At the end of the year, I tried one more time. Texting him seemed pointless, but I tried anyway. I texted him saying I was thinking about him and looking forward to grabbing lunch soon. I placed my phone down and came running back when I heard it vibrate. His response shattered my world.

"Jordan, it is good to hear from you. I'm sorry I haven't responded. I have been in jail for the last 90 days for some DUI charges. I want you to know I found God in the cell. I have never been happier in my life. Let's talk soon."

Once again I shouted, "SERIOUSLY, GOD!?" But this time it was a shout filled with joy. I began dancing around the apartment, receiving a few glares from my wife. God had worked wonders in the life of a man I never thought would pursue Him. God had taken this man and changed his life.

I started receiving texts from Connor about how he was praying for me and looking forward to coming and hearing me preach. Who was this man? Who was this person who texted me before finals saying he was praying for me to do well? Whoever he was, God used me in some minor way to change his life. All I needed to do was be his friend.

This was not an easy journey—and it wasn't short either. You may be in a similar situation. I want you to know that it took five years of simply being Connor's friend for him to be open to what Jesus had in store for him. For others, it may take longer. If you are walking with someone and it has been twenty years, do not give up. God has something big in store for them. We cannot pursue and love others when we have an agenda. Simply be their friend and walk with them throughout their lives. God will open up doors in His timing and transform lives through the seeds we plant with our actions of love and compassion.

Leaving an Impact

I approached the stage as nervous as ever. I was gearing up to encourage a traditional, elderly church to launch a sports ministry. There was a hole in our community that needed to be filled, and I felt like this was the next step. Every day of the week, a group of five to ten kids from the neighborhood would gather on our property and play basketball. For years, the church had allowed anyone and everyone to come and play sports on their property, but never went out to build relationships with them. Impact Sports was a ministry to change that.

I obediently prepared the pitch, walked on stage, and watched God work. The community started donating money and gave the church resources to launch a sports ministry. I took the funds to Walmart, bought a basketball hoop and equipment, and went to work. Impact Sports was going to start the upcoming Wednesday and I was ecstatic about what God was going to do for our community. After setting up tables, a concession area, a sound system, and sports equipment, we prayed earnestly for God to use our church for His Kingdom. We weren't sure how this ministry would go but we believed God was going to use Impact Sports for something powerful. Once we were fully set up and ready to go, we anxiously waited for kids to show up. To make a long story short, only three kids ended up coming to play basketball—all of whom were grandkids of congregants at the church. Week after week, this was the same narrative. Every once in a while we added a kid or two and then never saw them again. We did not see a single kid from the community the entire month of June and could not understand what was going wrong.

Something needed to change.

Starting in July, I decided to only set up music and sports equipment. We kept the concessions inside, didn't lay out any tables, and only kept a few chairs out for friends and family members to sit and watch. We created an environment that wasn't structured and had zero expectations...

And they came. One by one we saw a community of kids gather around to play basketball. It blew me away. Everything I had known about structure and organizing a successful sports ministry was irrelevant. We started doing the same thing week after week and began putting names with faces. Five, ten, fifteen, twenty kids showed up to play basketball. Relationships started to form and bridges were being built. Our church was pursuing the community in the capacity that *the community* felt comfortable. It is insane to see what the Church is capable of when we tear down the walls of structure and expectations and meet people with *Shattered Windows & Pointless Dreams* where they are, over there, in their comfort zone.

Child after child was impacted in a positive way that summer. Relationships were formed and the ministry thrived. For three months we were blessed with the opportunity to engage with the community. After months of diving deep into earning their trust, these same kids started attending the church youth group events. We didn't even have to invite them. Every single time they saw our Impact Sports volunteers outside, they would run over and hang out with us. Christ was using us to leave an everlasting impact on their lives, and it started with getting uncomfortable and pursuing the community around us the way they needed us to.

Room 24: Written by Hospital Chaplain Lydia Miller

I asked a dear friend of mine to share a story from her experience as a hospital chaplain—a job that requires her to love people who have different beliefs than her. Her story is powerful and one I hold on to. I am grateful for Lydia's example of love.

"One beautiful Saturday, halfway through my shift, I was paged to the Emergency Department of our large hospital. Stroke

Team Activate, Level 1—the most severe and critical. As I descended via the back elevators, thoughts swirled in my mind. Would the patient be young? Would there be a family? How could I best reach out and minister? I prayed silently as the elevator approached the ground floor and I made my way to Room 24.

"As I stood outside the door and listened to the medics' report, I learned this young Burmese gentleman had called 911 himself. In broken English, he stated that he was not well and was in desperate need of help. By the time the EMTs arrived at his apartment, he was unconscious. After giving the report, the medics looked over at me. In an all too familiar scene, they informed me that the family had been present at the patient's home when he had fallen ill and were en route to the hospital. The nurses, techs, and physicians worked at a feverish pace— silently, urgently. Though I have no formal medical training, I knew the 'rhythm of the room' indicated the critical nature of this patient.

"Time is fleeting and precious, but it was even more so on that fateful afternoon in Room 24. I prayed quietly at the bedside as I carefully and mindfully attempted to stay out of the way of those who worked so desperately to save this young man's life. The results of the STAT medical tests began to pour in and the news was grim. Additional scans were ordered and the neurosurgeon was called in. My phone rang. It was the nurse at Triage calling to let me know that the family of the patient had arrived. I continued to pray for guidance and wisdom as I walked quickly to our Emergency Entrance and escorted the patient's wife and young daughter back to the Consult Room.

"Oat Aw, the patient's wife, was beautiful. Though terrified, she was gentle and soft-spoken. She, too, spoke very little English, and my heart broke at the news she would soon receive. Oat's sister and teenage nephew arrived. As they settled in and waited to speak to the neurosurgeon, I thought of how to best show the love of Jesus to this hurting little family. I offered water, tissues, and showed them to the restroom. I found new books to distract the little girl who, sensing her mother's anxiety, was in distress. This sweet little girl had no comprehension of the severity of the situation and she wanted to go to the library and read as had been the family's plan for the day. I asked if they had a clergy member I could contact. Through tears and a few words, Oat told me she and her husband were Buddhist. I offered to call the monk from the local Buddhist temple and we waited in silence together.

"When the neurosurgeon arrived and delivered the devastating news that Oat's husband had a brain bleed and was dying, I knelt before her and offered to hold her hands. The surgeon followed suit and knelt alongside me. Oat began to shake. Though we could barely communicate with her at that moment, the doctor and I told her how very sorry we were. She threw her arms around me and wept like a child. I held her gently and allowed her to cry.

"Three days later, after additional tests, the patient was declared brain dead. A Buddhist ceremony was held at the bedside. I was asked to attend and I stood in a corner and prayed for Oat and her little girl. After the ceremony was over, I asked if I could wrap Oat in a warm quilt and cover her husband with another. Once again, I held Oat as she wept, tears pouring from her eyes. Hours later, Oat's husband was removed from the ventilator and the cardiac time of death was called. Oat and her little daughter left our hospital, broken by the devastating loss of a wonderful husband and father.

"Several months later, our hospital held a memorial

service for all of those who had lost loved ones in our facilities over the past six months. As we prepared for the service, I saw a young woman enter the church doors. She hesitated at first, but then saw me. She rushed into my arms and the tears came, slowly at first, then in streams. Over and over, she repeated, "Thank you, thank you" and over and over, I gently wiped her tears and repeated, "I am so sorry, I am so sorry." It was a tender moment. A sacred moment. I held her for what seemed like an eternity. Then, ever so slowly, she turned and faced the church sanctuary. With a soft sigh, she squared her shoulders, went in and sat down. Her family and young daughter arrived and sat next to her in a pew in the back of the United Methodist Church, where we conduct our non-denominational memorial services.

"Suddenly, I was overcome with tears. It dawned on me that Oat was here—at a church, surrounded by people of different ethnicity and culture, listening intently to a Christian service in a language she barely understood. I was struck by the power of the love that connected her to this place. In spite of all of our differences, she came—out of love for her husband and out of gratitude for the love and respect we had shown her while her husband was in the care of our hospital. Oat stepped out of her comfort zone and into a different faith because she experienced love and hope.

"Oat and her little daughter experienced the love of Jesus. Love that heals. Love that brings cultures together. Love that doesn't exclude because of religion. Love that demonstrates His love for people and situations that are very different. Love that doesn't need words, just a quiet comforting presence. Love that shows His love, but doesn't have to speak it loudly. On that day, in Room 24, the Gospel message was shared, but not in the way many of us are taught. Often, our focus is on praying the right words, having the correct Scriptures in front of us, laying out the plan of salvation. But that isn't always possible in hospital chaplaincy. Patients and families don't often look like us, sound like us, believe like us. In those dark moments, we strive to meet the patient's needs exactly where and how they are. We are called to be the hands and feet of Jesus to all. While it wasn't in the traditional way, Oat and her little family "heard" the Gospel message loud and clear that Saturday afternoon, displayed in simple acts of kindness and a genuine love for all of God's children."

From *Them* to *Us*

Jesus viewed everyone as equals when He pursued them with love. Jesus did not categorize individuals based on their poor choices or their lifestyles. Jesus was more concerned about loving everyone than anything else. He challenged an oppressive religious system that for centuries had been neglecting "them." We cannot pursue a *"Jesus model"* without pursuing an *"Us model."* We are all one body. Paul describes it like this:

"For just as the body is one and has many members, and all the members of the body, though many, are one body, so it is with Christ. For in one Spirit we were all baptized into one body —Jews or Greeks, slaves or free —and all were made to drink of one Spirit (1 Corinthians 12:12-13, ESV)."

We were all made to worship God in unity. If we are having a difficult time welcoming others into our lives, the problem is not with others, but with us. Try pursuing the least, the lost, the lonely, and the forgotten, without an agenda.

Chapter 3: When Convictions Meet Contradictions

"The best of us must sometimes eat our words."

- Albus Dumbledore, Harry Potter and the Chamber of Secrets,

by J.K. Rowling

I have a confession to make. I struggle with something called "I am always right" syndrome.

Exhale. I said it.

I don't understand why everyone else doesn't understand I am always right. There are only two options: My way, and the wrong way. Does anyone else have this syndrome?

All "jokes" aside, this begs me to ask some questions: When convictions meet contradictions, how do we show love? When individuals are living a lifestyle or pursuing something we do not agree with, how do we respond? We are supposed to share truth... right?

Yes, we are supposed to share truth. But how we share truth seems to be the line many individuals disagree on. For some, showing endless amounts of grace and sharing zero truth is the way to handle these situations. For others, sharing 100 percent truth and no grace is the way to handle these situations. Some people go as far as wanting to play judge, jury, and executioner when these situations arise, and some act as though only their opinion matters. Some embrace everyone unconditionally, while some push back on different lifestyles and sins publicly. Some individuals are very good at posting their views on Facebook, and some are very good at staying silent.

I do not believe there is a 100 percent correct way to disagree with others, but there are definitely incorrect ways. Whenever I am approached with a sin or lifestyle that I do not agree with, I have to monitor my heart. Often, I will take a step back in order to ensure I handle every situation in 100 percent grace and in 100 percent truth. When my convictions come face to face with contradicting views, the best way to respond is always in grace *and* truth; it cannot be one or the other. With that being said, I will never allow a conviction of mine to override my call to serve everyone. I love how social justice activist Carlos A. Rodriguez defines our role as Christ-followers:

"If you want to flip tables like Jesus, make sure you're

also willing to die on the cross for the people sitting there."

We have permission to share Truth with other people. In fact, we are called to share Truth with others (see Romans 1:16) —but only if we are going to show them grace and are willing to die for them as Jesus did. This is why I lean towards sharing my convictions through my *actions*, not just my *words*. Some might say it is cowardly. I say it takes more courage and love to *show* everyone the life of Jesus than it does to point them to parts of Scripture they are most likely familiar with.

The Great Debaters

One of my passions has always been communication. I love learning how to communicate effectively and efficiently with others. Along with this, I love public speaking. While in high school, I was on my school's speech and debate team for four years and even qualified for the National Debate Tournament. My debate partner and I were best friends, even though we were very different. He was intelligent and knew something about everything. I could speak well... and that was about it. There would be times throughout our debate competitions he would hand me pieces of paper with things to say scribbled on them, and I would have no clue what he was talking about. Our game plan actually worked pretty well. I knew how to speak well, and he understood what I was saying—even if I didn't.

After I graduated high school, we stayed in contact. He was a year younger than I was, so he still had one more year to compete on the debate team. I had numerous opportunities to go back home and travel with the team as they competed during my holiday breaks. I had almost as much fun judging at competitions as I did competing in them.

Jason and I were not only different as far as intelligence goes, but spiritually we had different views as well. Jason was a devoted Catholic and I am a non-denominational Protestant. We disagreed on quite a few areas but never allowed our disagreements to impact our relationship. Trust me, with two debate partners going head to head on spiritual topics, things could get pretty heated, but we always placed the value of our *relationship* over the value of being *correct*.

During my sophomore year of college, I received a Facebook message from Jason. It read like this:

"Idk if you know, but I did finally come out as bisexual.

There was only one person in our friend group that knew. I'm having a tough time with the concept of being a Catholic and bi... it's hard loving God, but being told He hates you [and that] you are a mistake."

After reading it, I was crushed. I could have taken the opportunity to debate him, but instead, I responded like this: *"Yeah, I didn't hear, but it doesn't surprise me. No judgment here. I had actually been wondering for a while if you were bisexual, and it never has changed how I thought about you or cared about you."*

And that was it. That's all I have said about the subject matter. Some of you may disagree with how I responded to the situation. Some of you may have responded differently, and that is okay. For me, maintaining a relationship is more important than sharing my convictions 100 percent of the time. Jason already knows what the Church's stance is on bisexuality. What Jason didn't know was that God still loves him regardless. When I see Jesus approached by people with different lifestyles, His first response is one that helps them recognize the baggage in their lives without condemning them. Sometimes Jesus would encourage them or challenge them with questions, but He always loved them. This verse is significant enough to share twice in this book:

> *"A new command I give you: Love one another. As I have loved you, so you must love one another. By this everyone will know that you are my disciples, if you love one another (John 13:34-35, NIV)."*

We often want to only use our voice to share the Truth of God. God calls us in a new command to show individuals Truth through our actions. I find responding this way is a much more freeing way to follow Jesus. Does this mean we aren't honest in our views? Absolutely not. Does this mean we can't share our hearts? Absolutely not—but our response always needs to be loving. Do not try to convince or shame someone into believing they are living in sin. Trust me, speaking from experience, I can say that this type of response only leads to hate and destruction. Show others through your actions that God's grace is bigger than any conviction you may have. *Also, we could always be wrong about our convictions.*

Isn't that a tough pill to swallow?

* * *

Truth in Love

I believe God's grace is bigger than any sin someone may be pursuing. Some of you may not think same-sex marriage is a sin, and there is no judgment from me because of that either. Whether we agree or disagree is not the point. We should all be working towards the same response. Jason knows my belief on the subject —but he also understands that my love for him, and more importantly, God's love for Him has not changed because of it. I was broken when I found out Christ-followers had called Jason a mistake and condemned him to hell. Those beliefs and values do not line up with the God I follow.

I believe God is bigger than any conviction I have. I believe God is the only one with the ability to dictate a person's future. My obligation is to show everyone love, and when the opportunity presents itself, share my heart in a pure way with them about the Truth and the God I believe in. At the same time, I will never shy away from sharing my heart if someone approaches me and asks what I believe. If someone initiates the conversation, I will always respond, but only while standing firm in grace *and* in truth. I often think of it this way: Be firm in your conviction but filled with grace in how you respond to those who disagree. We do not know what kind of life or what kind of pain the person we are responding to may have experienced.

God Knows the Full Story

Before we respond aggressively towards sex before marriage, maybe we consider that the individual asking the question was sexually abused. Before we respond negatively towards drugs and alcohol, maybe we consider that the individual grew up with a family who struggles with drugs and alcohol abuse. Before we tell a child their dad is going to hell because he doesn't love God, maybe we should consider that the child's dad may have already died—his child only wants assurance he will see him again. Before we respond, we should always consider the heart behind the question, and then back it up with a pure-hearted response.

Only God knows the full story. This is why He gave us a command that will work throughout any circumstance presented to us. Not everyone who asks these questions or struggles with these things will have these stories listed above. If we respond with a pure heart, it won't matter.

When we pursue the least, the lost, the lonely, and the forgotten, our convictions are going to be challenged quite often.

When this happens, remember: Be firm in your conviction, but filled with grace in how you respond to those who disagree. If your conviction over a sin overrides your call to love others without an agenda, then your conviction is wrong. When convictions meet contradictions, choose to respond with grace, truth, and a whole lot of love.

Chapter 4: Hope in the Hallway

"You can't be against bullying without actually doing something about it." - Randi Weingarten

We used to learn about two school shootings when practicing our active shooter drills in grade school: Columbine and Virginia Tech. I remember watching videos specifically about these two schools as our teacher blasted us with information about how we needed to respond if a shooter entered the premises.

Today, schools are talking about the shooting that happened last week.

Across the street.

The next state over.

Or down the hall.

In different clubs or churches.

In different streets and houses.

It seems as though all someone has to do is turn on a television or radio to learn that another mass shooting has tragically taken place. The shooter often uses the excuse that they took someone's life because of their victim's sexuality or beliefs, but the true reason people murder others is that their heart is filled with hate. My heart was ripped apart as I waited for updates on the shooting in New Zealand this year that slaughtered fifty people and left fifty more injured because they were worshiping in a mosque. My heart was suffocating with its beat as I tried to slow my breathing down and attempt to comprehend how someone could do something so evil and sinful. While the shooting was devastating beyond words, the responses I saw from Christians were also heartbreaking...

"What's even worse is that none of those who died are going to Heaven."

"This is why we need stricter gun laws."

"This is why we don't need stricter gun laws."

"The shooter better be going to hell for what he did."

Are we God? Do we get to decide who goes to hell and who goes to Heaven? Are we the dictators and deciders of God's grace? Is pushing our political party's agenda more important than grieving with our neighbors? Why do we continue to damage grieving communities by our arrogance? Why do we continue to push individuals away from God with our law-based theology? Why do our Facebook posts spew out the very same evil that we are speaking out against?

A Broken Record

It breaks my heart that a chapter like this has to exist. It breaks my heart when I turn on the news and see another life was taken because of a senseless tragedy. It breaks my heart when I witness another media source taking advantage of the grief of others in order to advance their views. It makes me cringe when I see another individual post on Facebook, pushing views that don't invite conversation. I am a firm believer that many of the issues we are facing in our country do not have one answer.

Should we improve our gun control laws? Yes.

Should we promote anti-bullying campaigns? Yes.

Should we upgrade security in schools? Yes.

Should we check the intentions of our hearts? Yes.

Should we analyze how we are loving people? Yes.

When we dive into the brokenness of *Shattered Windows & Pointless Dreams* of others, it not only includes those with whom we disagree, but also those we do not even know. I walked into a high school not too long ago and it made me sick to see how teenagers were treating one another in the hallways.

Judgment.

Hate.

Arrogance.

Bullying.

And yet, nothing changes with adults. I see adults posting on social media their views about everyone they disagree with. It breaks my heart to see that the biggest divide in our country is caused by how we treat others. How will restoration begin if we continue to drive people away from God?

I am not immune to these descriptions. I constantly have to check myself. I am always watching what I post and what I share on social media to ensure that I do not target anyone in a hurtful way. As I recall my years in middle school and high school, I painfully regret how I treated classmates. There were days when I would bully, taunt, and arrogantly look down upon peers who were different than me to gain attention. I was insecure about my own flaws and would react by targeting people with similar experiences to feel peace.

When I was growing up, there was a student who was part of my friend group who had a few learning disabilities and extreme ADHD. Day after day, this kid was bullied for something weird he did or something unusual he said. Unfortunately, I was a big part of mistreating this individual. When your closest peers become your greatest negative influence, looking for hope in the hallways is unimaginable. Somehow this person continued showing up to school every day, even though he was bullied for who he was. This narrative is the case for many students walking through the halls of schools across the world today. The sad thing is that bullying is not self-taught, it is learned. Many of our youth witness how adults mistreat one another in their disagreements. Whether it is through gossip at the dinner table, offensive stances on social media, road rage, or discussing politics, our kids are soaking in every single thing we say and do. When we mistreat or abuse people through our words and actions, it sends off the signal that it is natural to hurt individuals with *Shattered Windows & Pointless Dreams*.

Some of the most popular people I know are individuals who sat at the lunch table with the "outsiders" at school. Young leaders whom everyone wanted to be around because they felt accepted and important. Individuals who brought hope to the hallways of classrooms and grocery stores because they were more concerned about helping everyone than being popular. People whom I desperately wish I could go back in time to and model my actions after.

Students seem to be struggling now more than ever. My prayer is that bullies put away their harsh words and actions and start including everyone. My prayer is that the hallways of schools are filled with hope rather than insults. My prayer is that students start looking out for one another rather than forcing others to change who they are in order to be accepted. Dreams of students are being shattered because they are taught at a young age that they have no worth. What would it look like for us to pursue the lives of students through empowerment, encouragement, and by believing in them?

Where Hope Meets Action

I ended up reaching out to my friend from grade school I used to bully. I apologized for everything I had done and made sure that he knew he was loved and I was proud of him. I was proud of him for not giving up even though his peers made him feel contemptible. I made sure I did not make any excuses and that he understood I was completely at fault for my actions. I ended by asking him if he would be willing to grab lunch and reconnect. Even though he had no reason to give me another chance in his life, he graciously accepted my apology and we ended up having lunch the next week.

I wish I could go back and change the way I treated my peers. Once I entered college, I, like most people, realized "rank" and "popularity" didn't matter. In college, I was amazed to see how often my friends would welcome everyone to hang out. It did not matter how weird you were or how different you seemed to be. I actually believe I would have been a lot less stressed and anxious in grade school if I had stopped worrying about what other people thought of me.

If you are a student, do not give up on yourself. If you are being bullied, or are the bully, don't give up on yourself.

If you are being bullied, I want you to know you are loved. I know it may not feel that way at the moment, and you may feel lonely and lost, but there is a God who calls you child (see 1 John 3) and has your back. A God who flipped tables because religious folk were abusing His temple cares for you (see Matthew 21). Do not think for a second He wouldn't do the same for you. I know now that I bullied students because I was insecure. It does not make it okay, but often shattered people shatter people. I encourage you to find someone in your life you can trust. As difficult as it is to brush off the haters, I encourage you to stand firm and believe you do have a purpose. Your life is not pointless and your dreams are valid. Do not give up because others haven't found security in who they are yet. *You need to believe in you.*

If you are a bully, do not make the same mistakes I did and wait until after college to reconcile with the people you may have hurt. Do not hesitate to change the way you treat those around you. I know that more often than not, we bully because we are experiencing pain ourselves. There are healthier ways to address our anger and our pain. Do not bring people down in order to elevate yourself. Just like I suggested earlier, I encourage all of us to find someone we can trust. Find somebody who sees the good in you and will encourage you and lift you up. Tomorrow, I challenge you to apologize to everyone you have mistreated. Seek humility and pursue grace. We will see the difference it makes in others and in ourselves.

Adults, it is time for us to rise up against the evil we are teaching our children to embrace. We may spend years waiting for legislation to be passed. We may spend countless hours praying for change to occur in the heart of our shattered world. Let's also be the example the youth need. Let's set the standard for our children to love everyone regardless of their differences. Let's teach our kids to be a classmate who invites everyone to eat lunch with them. Let's set an example of what it looks like to fill students with hope in the hallways. Every child has a story. Every teenager has a dream. Let's play an active role in teaching our kids to empower one another in their stories and in their dreams. Have a conversation with your child regardless of how innocent they may be. Teach your children to treat everyone fairly and with grace, and then set the example by doing the same. Our hallways are shattered, but it does not have to be this way. There is hope for the lockers, classrooms, and lunch tables... and it starts with us.

Chapter 5: Get Back to Your Burdens

"The fellowship of true friends who can hear you out, share your joys, help carry your burdens, and correctly counsel you is priceless." - Ezra Taft Benson

There I was, sitting in silence in my bedroom. Anxiety had attacked me yet again and I felt helpless. My heart was beating rapidly and my mind was racing all over the place. I had trouble focusing and thinking about the tasks at hand. Quietly, I felt a tempting whisper linger through my mind...

Get back to your burdens....

I spent the next five minutes rocking back and forth. For the past six months, I have dealt with anxiety attacks beyond control. I have switched medications four different times, been to counseling, spent time in prayer, and still wake up anxious. Anxiety was always something I struggled with growing up, but never like this. I feel as though there is a breastplate of anxiety placed on my chest I cannot take off. Every day, I attempt to rip away from its power, and yet, this small whisper continues to remind me of my pain…

Get back to your burdens.

Get back to your burdens. It is a phrase we see Pharaoh tempting Moses and Aaron with after Moses finally builds up the courage to approach Pharaoh head-on. It is a phrase we see the enemy use against many of us when we begin the journey of pursuing individuals who are shattered and described as a pointless pursuit. While it may seem challenging and necessary to go back to your burdens, it is often a tool the enemy uses for us to go back to comfort.

Get back to your own life.

My dad used to tell me every time the enemy was close, God was closer. However, the enemy is still close — tempting us to ignore our calling, minimize our influence, and pursue ourselves. We see an example of this in Exodus:

> *"But the king of Egypt said to them, "Moses and Aaron, why do you take the people away from their work?* **Get back to your burdens."** *And Pharaoh said, "Behold, the people of the land are now many, and you make them rest from their burdens (5:4-5 ESV)!"*

Just like Pharaoh was trying to tempt Moses and Aaron to ignore their calling, one of the most effective ways satan can tempt us is through comfort.

Isolate yourself.

Pursue your own life.

You have too much on your plate to worry about the needs of others.

Your anxiety is too powerful.

Do you really think you are worthy of caring for your neighbor?

Get back to your burdens...

I struggle with finding the balance between serving others and taking care of myself. Anxiety makes this challenging because the people I am passionate about serving are also the ones who require the most energy. One of my greatest fears is the fear of loss. I am constantly worrying about my family and whether or not I am going to see them again. Has this fear prevented me from caring for others in times of need? How much power do I give my anxiety? How much power do I give my pain? How much power do I give my burdens? These are the questions I have to wake up and wrestle with every single day.

What is it for you? What is your fear? What is your comfort? What is your itch that keeps you from scratching other areas? What is your *burden*?

Self-Care

I mentioned earlier I struggle to find the balance between taking care of myself spiritually and investing in the lives of others. It is so important that we do both in balance so we do not burn out. I am the type of person who finds it impossible to slow down and rest. I realize my anxiety increases on days I do less. This is why the concept of taking a Sabbath is difficult for me to understand. A Sabbath is a command found in the Hebrew Bible and then reiterated throughout the New Testament as a day of complete rest. If God created the Heavens and the earth in six days and rested on the seventh, we should rest as well.

However, I believe the definition of rest is different from person to person. In fact, it *needs* to be different for each person. The goal of the Sabbath is to find joy through things that provide rest for us. God has already overcome the world (see John 16:33), so it is important for us to spend a day resting and adoring the Overcomer. For some, this means binge-watching Netflix all day—that would drive me crazy. Some people find rest by dividing their day into sections—one hour spent doing time alone with God, one hour shopping, one hour reading, one hour with friends, and so on and so forth. Some sleep all day and others do something around the city. I don't believe rest is the same for everyone, but I do believe it is important for everyone to rest—especially when navigating through our burdens and the burdens of others. It is crucial we take time to do things that refuel us. We cannot expect to carry the burdens of others if we do not spend time resting and giving our burdens to God. Here are some things that have helped my restless soul find rest so I have the energy and motivation to help others:

1. **Find a hobby separate from your job.** When I am battling anxiety or fear, I slow down by doing things I love. It is important that these hobbies be separate from our job or our work because it is difficult for us to shut off our working mind and rest when our mind is still working on tasks at hand. Taking an hour to do something that brings joy has helped me quite a bit. I love writing, reading, playing video games, and hanging out with

friends. On Mondays, which are my days off, I make sure I do all four of these things at different points throughout the day. Even though I am still doing hobbies that require energy, I am refueled, fully rested, and ready to go for Tuesday because I spent a day resting with things that bring me joy. Now, these things do not completely take away my anxiety, but they give me the energy to combat my anxiety. Whatever you are struggling with, whether it be an internal struggle or an external struggle, I encourage you to enter the battlefield by doing things that bring you joy.

2. **Let friends or family members know when you are struggling.** I cannot stress enough how important this is. We are not designed to do life alone. Even Jesus reached out to His friends when He was struggling (see Matthew 26:36). If you're anything like me, then this is something you may have a hard time doing. I used to be terrible at telling my wife when I was anxious. As of late, I have started texting her whenever I feel anxious so she can pray for me. Even though it is challenging for me to be

vulnerable with people, I find when I let others know my weaknesses, God uses them to give me strength.

3. **Let God know.** This may seem pointless because God knows everything, but it actually helps. And God appreciates our vulnerability. The power of prayer cannot be overstated. As in any relationship, communication is essential. If we want a healthy relationship with God then we need to communicate with God. No matter where I am, if I am feeling anxious, I take a few moments to pray. I always start out by thanking God for another breath and then ask Him to calm my spirit. Sometimes I feel it work immediately; sometimes I don't. But I know God does not abandon me, even if it feels that way. Faith often feels like getting hit by a semi-truck and then choosing to get back up even though the next one is in sight. I choose to always get back up. God is never going to forsake me, even in the moments I feel alone. Spend time praying and asking God for His presence to be known—and then on the days He feels absent, hold on until the morning.

* * *

Carry Each Other's Burdens

Our burdens are 100 percent significant. Our struggles, sufferings, pains, and hardships are extremely important to focus on... but so are those of others. We cannot spend all of our energy focusing on ourselves and call it "self-care." As I mentioned earlier, it is important that we reach out to people when we are struggling. At the same time, it is also important that we reach out to people who are struggling. Think about the days you feel alone. Think about the days you feel anxious. Do you have someone you know is willing to drop what they are doing to talk with you or be with you? Are you that way with other people? If I spend most of my energy working through my fears and my burdens, and the rest of it attempting to self-care, I miss out on the goodness and beauty for which God has created me. Finding the balance between caring for myself and serving others is something I'm still trying to figure out, but it is not either/or. We cannot have one without the other. God created us to be in community (see Proverbs 27:17). The enemy will try to isolate us in our pain, but God says our burdens all need to be connected. Paul paints the picture beautifully in his letter to the church in Galatia:

"Carry each other's burdens, and in this way you will fulfill the law of Christ (Galatians 6:2, NIV)."

Just like Paul carried the burdens of different churches, I have a friend who has always cared for the needs of others. This person is known for how he cares for other people in the midst of their burdens. He jumps at any opportunity to serve others. But at the same time, he is still weak at moments and needs others to walk with him. Life was designed to be lived in community. We cannot put our own needs over the needs of others. We cannot grant our burdens power over our lives. Declare war against your circumstance, and push onward towards others.

This is why Jesus firmly shares that we were created to help others in Luke:

In reply Jesus said: "A man was going down from Jerusalem to Jericho, when he was attacked by robbers. They stripped him of his clothes, beat him and went away, leaving him half dead. A priest happened to be going down the same road, and when he saw the man, he passed by on the other side. So too, a Levite, when he came to the place and saw him, passed by on the other side. But a Samaritan, as he traveled, came where the man was; and when he saw him, he took pity on him. He went to him and bandaged his wounds, pouring on oil and wine. Then he put the man on his own donkey, brought him to an inn and took care of him. The next day he took out two denarii and gave them to the innkeeper. 'Look after him,' he said, 'and when I return, I will reimburse you for any extra expense you may have (Luke 10:30-35, NIV).'

Most read this story as a call to help others in need. While this is true, my ministry practicum at Anderson University showed me that there is more going on. Here are some things to note about the good Samaritan:

1. The walk from Jericho to Jerusalem was exhausting and deadly. However, the journey was necessary if the communities wanted to trade with other areas. Individuals would venture on the journey in order to provide for their families and their communities.

2. Temple laws found in the books of Exodus, Leviticus, and Numbers are what stopped the priest and the Levite

from helping the Jew (see Numbers 19:11). They were more concerned about being deemed "unclean" than they were about loving people. As we read through the Hebrew Bible today, it makes sense why the priest and the Levite did not aid the Jew. There are plenty of "Jews" today that many of us pass by. If we are being honest with ourselves, most of us are no different than the priest or the Levite.

3. The Jews and Samaritans hated one another. There is a history of evil and violence between the two communities. This is why it is astonishing that the Samaritan is the person who stops to help the Jewish man. This begs us to ask ourselves, "Who is the person in our lives we hate the most? Would we stop and aid them if they were in need?"

4. The Samaritan is risking his safety by helping the man. If anyone from his community saw him helping a Jew, he could've been beaten or killed. His family could have faced the same consequences as well. However, the Samaritan pursues the burdens of another, regardless of their differences.

5. Not only does the Samaritan help the Jew in need, but he fully finances his recovery by making sure this man will receive the care he needs. Some of us might be willing to help someone initially, but are we willing to walk with them throughout their lives?

The story of the good Samaritan is so much more than a call to care for our neighbors in need. It is a call to place the burdens of others above our comfort, safety, finances, agenda, expectations, and differences. If God has called us to serve and love people, we cannot allow the enemy to tempt us with comfort. We cannot let the enemy remind us of our past. We cannot allow satan authority over our calling. Our burdens are very important, but we cannot use them as an excuse to ignore the burdens of others. God often uses our burdens and experiences to give hope to others in the midst of their burdens and experiences.

Where would we be if Moses had gone back to his burdens? What if the Samaritan had ignored the man on the side of the road? What if Paul had not planted and walked with churches across the world? What if Jesus had not placed the burdens of others on His back when He died on the cross?

Take a moment and pray. Pray about the burdens in your life. Pray about the wall that has been built in your life that needs to be taken down. Have a conversation with God about the people in your life who need help with their burdens. Life can feel very lonely when we are surrounded by the weight of burdens. This is why I challenge us to pursue others in their loneliness and walk with others in their fight for hope. Also, declare war against your own burdens. If it feels like your burdens are too heavy to carry, reach out to someone. Pass along your burdens to God and let your friends and family members walk with you. At some point in our lives, we all feel shattered. At some point in our lives, we all ask, "What's the point?" Do not let satan use your burdens against you during this time. Do not give your burdens power over the mission to pursue hope for yourself and bring hope to others.

My struggles will not define me. Your struggles will not control you. Whether we are battling an addiction, the loss of a loved one, a financial burden, an abusive relationship, a mental illness, an overwhelming schedule, or trying to figure out who God is, we are in this fight together to take back what the enemy has stolen. Fight the good fight, win back your life, and help others win back their lives. Try this today: Declare war against your burdens while bringing hope to others in the middle of theirs.

Chapter 6: Empowering the Powerless

"You can do what I cannot do. I can do what you cannot do.

Together we can do great things." - Mother Teresa

My wife Marissa and I were craving a church family that loved us and inspired us to move mountains. After getting married, we officially moved to Anderson, Indiana, to finish school. Leaving our church and families in Fort Wayne, Indiana, we embarked on a new journey in a city that was unfamiliar to us. Marissa and I had transferred to Anderson University the semester before and were still getting used to the ins and outs of the area.

One of the things we struggled with early on in our marriage was finding a church we could call home. We both grew up as pastors' kids and absolutely loved the church we attended back in Fort Wayne. Because we both had great experiences with one church our entire life, we really did not know what else was out there. We began looking for a church we could call home and searching for a place we felt welcomed and desired. Finding a church that would empower us to use our gifts and our passion for ministry was a necessary part of the process. However, it was also something that made the process very difficult. It is easy to find a church where we can be a number, yet it is very rare to find a church that will empower us in using our gifts for the Kingdom of God.

Church after church we attended and walked away feeling discouraged. There was nothing terribly wrong with any of the churches we checked out, but there was an unsettling feeling we felt after we left the service. After two months of checking out six different churches, we began to grow weary. My wife broke down crying numerous times because she was devastated she had to leave the church family she loved back home and could not find anything remotely close in Anderson to replace it. I remember feeling discouraged when school started up in August. Would we ever find a place to jump in and serve? A place to call home?

One of my classes was going to be taught by pastor Todd Faulkner (the author of the foreword). Pastor Todd had recently stepped down from being the campus pastor and was now entering into a full-time teaching role at the university. I had heard exceptional things about Pastor Todd and was excited to have him as a professor and mentor. It wasn't long before I fell in love with the way he explored the topics we were studying. He taught with passion and excitement. He was a storyteller bringing the Gospel to life. I would eventually go on to take five of his classes as electives because the way he portrayed Jesus was unlike any other person I had encountered. He even taught a Faith and Fantasy class covering the Harry Potter series and the Marvel Universe.

He. Was. Awesome.

A few weeks into the semester, pastor Todd shared something with our class that left me inching forward on my seat. He said, "For those of you that do not know, I am a part-time pastor at a small church in Chesterfield, Indiana. Originally we ran just one, traditional service. However, the elders have given me the green light to launch a second service called Encounter. The Encounter service will be student-led and geared towards empowering young adults to empower others. We are going to combine art, music, teachings, and interactive ideas in order to encounter Christ in new forms of worship. If any of you are interested in joining the team, please let me know and I will give you some information about a callout meeting after class."

I was hooked. Everything I had been wanting in a church had suddenly fallen into my lap. I hadn't even attended Chesterfield yet and already knew this would be the church home Marissa and I had desperately longed for. Without hesitation, I ran up to Pastor Todd and told him I was very interested in joining the team. I imagine I came across as weird and too energetic, but I hope he appreciated my enthusiasm.

Pastor Todd gave me the details for the callout meeting and invited Marissa and me to be a part of the Encounter Team. After the first meeting and service, we were sold on Pastor Todd's leadership. Todd and his wife Cindy, gave Marissa and I opportunities to use our gifts for God's glory on Sunday mornings and throughout the week. Every Sunday, we woke up filled with a new hope and a new type of energy. We actually enjoyed waking up early for church again. For the first time in a long time, we felt like we were at home worshiping with family.

A few months had passed and we were ready to step into a bigger leadership role. Marissa and I shared with Todd and Cindy that we had a desire to launch a young adult's small group for the college-aged community and a sports ministry for the youth in the community. We knew both ministries would be a huge jump for the church, but we believed God was calling us to pursue our neighbors with *Shattered Windows & Pointless Dreams*. Todd, Cindy, and the Encounter Service empowered me and Marissa to use our gifts. We were ready to start empowering others in the community.

Empower the Marginalized

Todd and Cindy always did an exceptional job of believing in others' potential. They rarely turned down an idea without discussing it further with the Encounter team and they always found ways to empower the marginalized in their strengths. They both saw the excitement that filled mine and Marissa's eyes when we shared our vision for the future with the small group and sports ministry, and they immediately gave us the green light to start something. While they couldn't commit to anything financially before talking with the church elder board, they both believed in us and our leadership to head up these two new ministries.

Marissa and I decided to start the small group the following semester. The group would be called "Move

Mountains," based on Matthew 17. The sports ministry would launch in the summer. We would spend one evening a week playing basketball and volleyball with underprivileged kids in the community. Marissa and I had zero expectations of what these ministries would look like or how they would turn out; but we truly felt like God, Todd, and Cindy, were empowering us to make a difference on our college campus and in our community.

God did not hesitate to use these ministries for His Kingdom. As I explained in chapter two, our sport's ministry, which we called Impact Sports, continued to grow and impact the lives of others in our community. Over the course of the next year, we were able to serve and empower twelve young adults in a weekly book or Bible study and build lifelong relationships. It was exciting to see God use Marissa and me to serve others. Every week, young adults and kids showed up to receive love and encouragement. We had cried out to God countless times for Him to help us find a church home we could get involved in. We had spent countless Sundays searching for a place we could call home. God honored our cries and placed us in a position to move mountains for His Kingdom. Todd and Cindy showed us how important it is for privileged individuals to step back and empower the marginalized. Society might call them a *pointless pursuit,* but God calls them *worthy leaders.*

The exciting thing about this entire story is that even though Marissa and I ended up moving away a year later to pursue ministry opportunities in Fort Wayne, the small group and sports ministry are still alive and well. While Move Mountains and Impact Sports look a bit different than the way Marissa and I led them, they are still being led by God to do amazing things. It was our goal to empower people in leadership to take over the ministries after we left. The last thing we wanted was to see the needs of the young adults and kids not be met because Marissa and I didn't find leadership to replace us after we were gone. Just like Todd and Cindy did with us, it was our mission to empower others to replace us and keep the ministries thriving.

Todd and Cindy impacted Marissa and I more than anybody else ever has in our life. They empowered us in our strengths and encouraged us in our weaknesses. They gave us opportunities to serve and use our gifts like nobody else ever has. They believed in us even when we felt hopeless. They challenged us when we felt discouraged. They empowered us when we were powerless.

You may be in a place of leadership.

You may have an opportunity to use your platform to empower others.

You may be financially well off and have the ability to bless other ministries in your reach.

We may be missing something in our lives. Something we cannot provide but somebody else can. A passion or an idea that others may only need the "green light" from us in order to move. Everyone in this world is gifted far beyond human comprehension. They may be waiting for somebody in leadership to empower them. In fact, it is our duty to empower individuals with *Shattered Windows & Pointless Dreams*.

You're Up

While reading this chapter, you may have felt your heart start racing. The truth is, you may be someone with an idea. You may be someone eagerly looking to use your gifts for God's Kingdom. You may be desperately crying out to God for opportunities and doors to open up for you to use your gifts. It is very discouraging to live in the *waiting game*. However, what appears to be a lack of movement from God is often a time period God is using for growth and character development.

While Marissa and I needed a place to serve, we had to do our part as well in the searching. Too often we expect God to place opportunities on our doorstep without any work being done on our end. I promise you, things like that rarely, if ever, happen. If you are eager to serve, pursue opportunities and serve. If you are able to empower, empower others in their gifts. If you are passionate about change, be the change that you hope to see. We need to start empowering the marginalized and those deemed shattered and pointless by society. God will do amazing things when we do our part. When the coach calls your name, don't hesitate to jump in the game.

I truly believe the way we show our neighbors we trust them, love them, and believe in them is by empowering them to do extraordinary things. Jesus empowered a group of misfits to do life with him. Calling twelve disciples with different sins, lifestyles, careers, gifts, and passions, Jesus created a team that would end up leading a revolution to change the world. The disciples were a group consisting of a tax collector, fishermen, a zealot, and a thief. Listen to how Matthew describes Jesus empowering His disciples in his Gospel:

"As Jesus was walking beside the Sea of Galilee, he saw two brothers, Simon called Peter and his brother Andrew. They were casting a net into the lake, for they were fishermen. "Come, follow me," Jesus said, "and I will send you out to fish for people." At once they left their nets and followed him. Going on from there, he saw two other brothers, James the son of Zebedee and his brother John. They were in a boat with their father Zebedee, preparing their nets. Jesus called them, and immediately they left the boat and their father and followed him (Matthew 4:18-22, NIV)."

Just like Jesus empowered the disciples to join the mission, we can empower others and take part in the revolution that is changing the world. Give the "least of these" opportunities to lead. If someone is passionate about something, help them find the best avenue to pursue that passion. Regardless of age, gender, race, sexual orientation, or religion, we must team up with our neighbors and start making a bigger difference in the world. I understand it can be very difficult to let others lead. If you are anything like me, you may be a bit of a control freak. Anytime I have an idea, I know exactly how I would execute it perfectly. The thought of allowing others the responsibility of leading often makes me cringe. But it is *necessary* to let others lead for Kingdom growth.

The other day I was part of the welcome team for our Saturday night service at church. I was in charge of passing out programs and welcoming everyone with a smile and a, "So glad you are here!" As I was getting started, a little six-year-old girl named Sarah was looking at me out of the corner of her eye. She had a huge smile on her face and I could tell she was intrigued by what I was doing. I decided to call her over and asked her if she would like to help me welcome people as they walked through the doors. Her face lit up with excitement. She could not believe she was being given such great responsibility. She ran over to the table, dropped off her granola bar, grabbed some programs, and immediately started welcoming people with excellence. I kid you not, I did not do a single welcome the rest of the night. I didn't have to; she was crushing being a greeter. She greeted every person walking through the door with a huge smile on her face and an enthusiastic, "So glad you are here!" She was filled with joy and filled others with joy as they walked in.

Age doesn't matter. Paul encourages Timothy not to allow anyone to look down on him because he is young (see 1 Timothy 4:12). We cannot look down on others because of their age or the potential *we see*. God takes our human expectations and shatters them. Can you imagine how angry God gets when we place limitations on others based on what we think they can accomplish? While it can be difficult to give up control, something as small as allowing others the opportunity to pass out a program can work wonders for the Kingdom. When we believe in others and empower them in their gifts we are spreading the love of Christ.

Some individuals feel powerless—empower them. Choose to take next steps towards giving others opportunities to use their gifts. God will do amazing things when we do.

Chapter 7: Masking Tape and a GoPro

"Where justice is denied, where poverty is enforced, where ignorance prevails, and where any one class is made to feel that society is an organized conspiracy to oppress, rob and degrade them, neither persons nor property will be safe."

- Frederick Douglass

Have you ever had a friend that was both passionate and kind of odd? The kind of person who would be willing to help you with anything but you have to understand that they may do it differently than you had envisioned? But at the same time, the kind of person who will always have your back and will consistently look out for the needs of others? I am lucky to have someone like this in my life.

I would like to introduce you to my friend Blake. Blake is in his twenties with a rock star beard, a bald head, and a passion for serving kids. I had the privilege of working with Blake at a facility called the Jam Center. The Jam Center is a community center located in Garrett, Indiana, with a heart for empowering others while providing a safe facility for families to exercise. Much like a YMCA, the Jam Center offers different aerobics classes, a huge gym, an early childhood education program, a swimming pool, and a teen program. Blake and I worked with the teen program. Every day of the week we had kids from the local middle schools come over to the Jam Center for an after-school program. Dinner was always provided, but the activities we did varied based on the theme for each week. We were a part of Club Jam on Tuesdays and Thursdays for both boys and girls, and Boys Club on Fridays.

One Friday during Boys Club, Blake and I finished cleaning up dinner and took the boys to the gym for scooter races. We had recently purchased a GoPro and wanted to start filming footage of the kids during activity time for future promotion videos. After we got all the scooters out, created the obstacle course, and opened the GoPro box, we were ready to go. Only one problem... the GoPro did not come with a headband. Either we did not order a GoPro headband, or we misplaced it. Regardless, we had no way of holding the GoPro steady on the kids' heads while they were scootering. Disappointed, we got the kids lined up in teams and passed out the scooter boards to begin the races. Right before we were about to start, Blake had an excellent idea. He told me, "Hold on a second, I'll be right back." Blake took the GoPro and ran out of the gym. Like I mentioned, Blake was a bit odd, so it was common for him to act on a crazy idea. However, the events that took place next completely shattered the way I viewed what it meant to live like Jesus.

Blake walked back into the gym with a huge smile on his face and the GoPro taped around his head with masking tape. His bald head now had a GoPro mounted on the top with layers and layers of tape. I completely lost it. The kids completely lost it. We were filled with joy as we saw how committed he was to serving the kids. He proved once again he would do anything to bring joy to his kiddos.

Blake showed me that day what it looks like to pursue everyone. Through his goofiness, he consistently brings joy to everyone he encounters. Blake, a Spiritualist, not even a Christian, showed me sometimes it takes masking tape and a GoPro to pursue our neighbors. No matter how ridiculous he looked, or how painful it was to take off the tape, he did not care.

All Blake cared about was serving everyone.

Pointless Pursuit

Many of the kids we have the privilege of working with at the Jam Center live in broken homes. According to the U.S. Census Bureau, as of 2017, 20.1 percent of Garrett, Indiana, lived in poverty. Many of these children live in single parent homes, have parents who are addicted to either drugs or alcohol, have experienced different levels of physical, verbal, and sexual abuse, and struggle with suicidal thoughts. Some are gay and some are transgender. Every single kid has a story filled with chapters and chapters of brokenness and baggage. Many individuals would write these kids off as a *pointless pursuit* because of the baggage they have and the way they act—but not Blake. Blake pursues every single one of those kids with grace and love because he truly believes their stories are not over. He believes they have a purpose for breathing. He knows their dreams are important and possible to achieve. Not only does he believe in them, but he empowers them to fulfill their dreams. Blake is helping put an end to generational poverty and abuse. I had the privilege of seeing him bring these kids hope—hope they would never have had without a mentor like Blake doing things like taping a GoPro to his head.

As I saw him hop on a scooter and take part in the scooter races with the kids, I was in awe. He was helping me see the point to Jesus' response in Mark,

> *"People were bringing little children to Jesus for him to place his hands on them, but the disciples rebuked them. When Jesus saw this, he was indignant. He said to them, "Let the little children come to me, and do not hinder them, for the kingdom of God belongs to such as these. Truly I tell you, anyone who will not receive the kingdom of God like a little child will never enter it." And he took the children in his arms, placed his hands on them and blessed them (Mark 10:13-16, NIV)."*

There is something powerful about pursuing the next generation in love. They may not act like you did during the "good ol' days," but they are the next people God is chasing after unconditionally. You may have people in your life who are EGR individuals (extra grace required)—give them extra grace through patience and self-control. You have no idea what kind of home life they have. Too often people have been counted out because of their past. If we don't start breaking the cycle of generational poverty, generational abuse, and generational addictions, we will never be able to bring hope to the least of these. According to research organized by the U.S Census Bureau, the official poverty rate in 2017 was 12.3 percent. That means that 39.7 million people in the United States were living in poverty. That is 39.7 million more than God desires. Along with this, according to Kids At Risk Action (KARA) Groups, one in four girls and one in six boys will be sexually abused before they turn eighteen. What are we doing to help those who are being abused?

At the Jam Center, we have one boy who was expelled from school last year because he threatened to shoot up the school. You can see the anger on his face when you are around him. He is easily triggered and very impatient, but in the midst of his baggage I see a kid who is aching to find joy. I see a kid who is broken inside and is crying out for help. I see a kid who desperately wants to find hope again. As difficult as it is to show this child grace, he is exactly who God calls us to pursue. He doesn't need to live a life filled with anger and hate.

Who is that person in your life?

Who is a child society has abandoned?

Who is someone who believes their story is over, but you know it is far from the conclusion?

I want to encourage us to start pursuing the next generation with love and grace. Start believing in them. Start empowering them. We need to play our part in ending generational poverty and generational brokenness. Start reaching out to teenagers with *Shattered Windows & Pointless Dreams* consistently, and give them opportunities to bounce back. If we are in a position of power, we need to help them in any way we can. If we are in a position of encouragement, we need to encourage them daily. If we are in a position of leadership, we need to let them lead. Some of the greatest leaders I know are teenagers. If we are in a position like Blake was, let's tape a GoPro to our head. Together, we can break the cycle of generational poverty, generational abuse, and generational addictions.

Chapter 8: Their Pain

"Friendship is born at the moment when one person says

to another, "What! You too? I thought I was the only one."

- C.S. Lewis

As I stated previously, I grew up as a PK. PK is slang us pastor's kids use when we address one another. It is almost like a code we have for each other. Kind of like how individuals who own Jeeps always wave at each other... I still think that is weird.

For those who are not pastor's kids, here are some characteristics that many of us have in common:

1. We always arrive first on Sunday mornings.

2. We always leave last after church.

3. We must be on our best behavior, even when every bone in our body wants to goof off with other teenagers (don't be fooled, I did not do this part very well).

4. We must always stand for worship and if we don't our parents will hear about it.

I remember one Sunday afternoon after church, my friends and I were wrestling in the gym. I had recently joined the wrestling team at my high school and my friends thought it would be a great idea to teach me some moves so I wouldn't get slaughtered my first match. That year of wrestling, I won one match and lost 24. Apparently, the advice my friends gave me was not the greatest. Anyways, as we were wrestling with each other, I remember my youth leaders running around the corner and yelling at us to stop. As you might imagine, wrestling on hard floors is not the safest thing to do.

Without thinking, I turned around and yelled, "If I weren't the pastor's kid you wouldn't care!"

Word of advice PK's, that response never works and never ends well.

While it sounds like a stressful gig to have, I actually enjoyed growing up as a pastor's kid. My dad was THE best pastor a son could ask for. Not only did he manage to go *all in* on every sermon, every single Sunday, but he found time to attend most of his kids' sporting events and take part in our lives without excuses. My dad only missed a few football games of mine in ten years of playing. My dad always put God first and his family second, no matter what his job required of him.

Along with supporting his family at our events, my dad also instilled in me a love for THE Michigan Wolverines. All of you Ohio Muckeye fans reading the book have permission to stop. There is not enough content in this book to help you out... just kidding. Well, sort of.

Michigan football was a big deal at my house. My dad made sure our family watched every game together and we had enough junk food to last us the entire weekend. We would grill burgers and wings and have desserts like caramel corn and Red Vines every game. My dad also took my brother and me to one Michigan football game and one basketball game a year. If you have never experienced the Michigan football stadium, also called "The Big House," then you have not really lived. The Big House is the largest football stadium in the United States, and one of the largest in the world. Walking into The Big House is like riding the roller coaster at Cedar Point, "The Millennium Force." *Exhilarating. Breathtaking. Exceptional.*

Because I had the privilege of doing life with my dad 24/7 (and trust me, it felt like 24/7), it was sometimes difficult for me to listen to him preach on Sunday mornings. Shamefully I can admit there were quite a few times I dozed off during one of his messages. Not because he wasn't doing well; I'm sure he was. It was because I was a teenage boy and that's what teenage boys do. With that being said, whenever my dad said something about a topic I really enjoyed, I would walk up to him afterward and thrust my arm forward and scream, "FIRST DOWN." This was something we would do to one another to imply we had once again moved the chains in our lives and the lives of others, and helped congregants take next steps with God.

One of my favorite sermons my dad delivered was the final message of a six-week-long "Follow" series. To close the series, he decided to do one of the bravest things I've ever seen him do... sing. To add some context, my dad was a terrible singer. Not only was he terrible but he had zero confidence whatsoever. Imagine an American Idol audition that could not get worse... well, my dad made it worse. Regardless, because my dad was willing to show the congregation that following Jesus meant doing things that would make us uncomfortable, he picked up the guitar and sang an amazing song...

"I have decided... to follow Jesus. I have decided... to follow Jesus. I have decided... to follow Jesus, no turning

back... no turning back."

Unfortunately, as soon as I started to appreciate who my Dad was and what he meant to me, life did a U-turn.

On December 17, 2013, the outreach pastor at our church, Brad Mattax, came to pick me up from work. I was working in the kitchen at the local Pizza Hut when I received the news my father had died from an unexpected heart attack. Undoing my seatbelt in Brad's car, I bolted out of the front seat and ran. I had no idea what I was supposed to be feeling. The man who had meant so much to me was gone.

No more football games. No more basketball games. No more jokes about him being my dad when we were in public. No more crazy dance-offs in Walmart. No more Monday Night Football games. No more yelling "First Down" after a move-the-chains-worthy sermon. No more hugs that nearly broke my glasses because of how hard he squeezed. No more hearing his footsteps while he was thudding around upstairs. No more ice cream runs. No more playing Halo together. No more late-night movies. My dad didn't get to see me get married, would never meet his grandkids, and would never see me graduate college. I truly believed God had made a mistake.

Everything that was normal was now shattered. Every dream my dad encouraged me to pursue now felt pointless. My dad was my number one encourager and supporter. How could I live without him?

I don't remember much from that night. Bits and pieces of memories hang with me, but one thing I remember clearly is the ride home. "You promised you would protect my family, God, so please do not abandon us. I trust that you will protect us." This was the prayer I repeated out loud as I was taken home to grieve with my family.

I was trembling, absolutely shattered. As a seventeen-year-old who had just lost his dad and was about to graduate high school and move on to college, I was lost. My dad wasn't just my father, but he was also my pastor. I not only lost someone who raised me to become the man I am today, but I lost someone I would approach with questions about faith. The pain of losing someone who believed in me more than I believed in myself seemed unreal. I entered into a journey of healing and began wrestling with questions about God. Questions such as:

If God is good, why did my father die?

If God is just, why does my life feel shattered?

If God is love, why do I feel abandoned?

Day after day, I felt depressed and abandoned. I skipped more days of school during my final semester of high school than I attended. I found myself pulling away from my friends and family. I stopped going to church and acted as though my faith in God were mere dust on a windowsill.

The next four years of college were filled with off-and-on feelings of anger and bitterness towards God. I exerted so much energy hating Him and never invested that energy towards finding true healing. I got to the place where my pain was numb and I naturally started burying it down deeper and deeper — never to be discussed or examined. The worst part is, I didn't even know I was doing any of this. If you'd asked me how my relationship with God was, I would've said it was stronger than ever. However, God knew my heart was broken and I was searching for hope elsewhere.

The Shack

It wasn't until my senior year of college that I decided I was ready to confront God head-on with my suffering. I began meeting with a counselor at my school. Up until this point I had been against counseling. In the past, I had tried three or four different counselors and didn't connect with any of them. I had tried multiple different medications for my anxiety and depression, and none of them seemed to help ease my pain. However, something stirred inside of me that I needed to give counseling one last try. My school provided counseling services for students year-round. Because I was a senior, this was my last chance to take advantage of these services. I decided to give it a try.

As you might imagine, I was terrified of walking into the counseling office for the first time. I had run from God for four years and was emotionally and physically drained. Walking into the counseling center and sitting on the sofa across from my counselor left me shivering. It wasn't until my counselor spoke that I felt peace.

"Hello, Jordan, my name is James. Tell me a little bit about yourself."

Have you ever heard the calmness in somebody's voice and felt like you were safe? That was my experience with James. I have never met an individual who was so real and authentic, and yet talked with an authoritative, calm voice. It was almost as if Jesus were sitting on the sofa next to me with a big smile on His face because He had personally sent James to walk with me. I exhaled, felt peace, and believed James would be able to help me on the road to find healing from my pain.

Session after session we wrestled with my pain. We attacked my suffering head-on and addressed my depression and anxiety. James did not shy away from any emotions or feelings, regardless of how irrational they were. No matter how I felt entering his office each day, he met me where I was and walked with me every step of the way. He even asked me what type of essential oil or candle scent I wanted to have in the room that day. During one of our sessions, James said something to me that hit home with my suffering.

"Jordan, you need to have a "shack experience" with God. You need to go to a place where you used to find the most joy with your dad, but since his passing, you have avoided it because of the pain it would bring. You need to go to that place and confront God head-on. Confront Him with your anger and your pain. Allow God to meet you at your shack."

The Shack is a book written by William P. Young that tells a story of a father who loses his daughter tragically. Receiving an invitation from God to meet Him for a weekend at the shack where his daughter died, the dad takes a step towards his pain and confronts God at the shack.

I was blown away. I knew exactly where I needed to meet God to address my pain. I started to feel my fists unclench and my heart open up. God was shedding light on my story, one breath at a time.

After that counseling session, my relationship with God became real. I was comfortable confronting God with my pain. I was confident God loved me and could handle any pain I was experiencing. From that moment on, I began to address God one-on-one. I wasn't scared to invite God to my shack. I wasn't scared to say a few swear words. I began healing for the first time because I was being *real* with God. I may have said things many would frown upon, but our confrontations have been beautiful and authentic. God is meeting me exactly where I am and showing me that there can be hope found in the middle of my pain. I did not have to stay where I was forever. In fact, my story of pain and brokenness is one of the best tools I have been blessed with to help others in their pain and their brokenness. God began helping me tell my story to others. He has given me opportunities to teach on the topic of suffering and has placed friends in my life who have had similar stories. Even though I deserted God in multiple ways, God has never deserted me—a truth that took me five years to believe.

While I am still broken and experiencing pain on every level, God has walked with me every step of the way and has shown me that my pain will not go unnoticed. Though I feel alone at times—we all do—I believe God never forgets about me. I would do anything to feel one more of my dad's hugs, but being held by God in the meantime is helpful. One of my chaplains from college said it perfectly: "God doesn't make things happen for a reason, God makes reason out of everything." I believe that is what Paul writes to the church in Rome:

"And we know that in all things God works for the good of those who love him, who have been called according to his purpose (Romans 8:28, NIV)."

God takes our broken situation and uses it for good. God takes our pain and uses it to provide healing for others. God takes our story and uses it to help individuals who are experiencing different chapters of life. I do not believe God caused my dad's death. I'm not sure why my dad died. Stressing about that provides more pain anyways. I do, however, believe God has responded to my pain. When we view God as a God who *responds* rather than a God who *causes* or *could have prevented* our suffering, healing becomes easier. I started to recognize all of the ways God has responded to my pain over the years. I believe God is still good and present in this world.

God Came Through

Have you ever read the story of Job in the Hebrew Bible? Job is an individual who is tested beyond belief. He loses everything. His family, his livestock, his servants, his house... everything. In the middle of his pain, he shares real and authentic feelings with God. At the end of the narrative, God blesses Job's latter part of his life far more than his former part. God took Job's broken situation, used it to bring hope for others, and then restored him to a better life than he had before.

My family is a living example of a Job story. After my dad died, my mom started to pursue God on new levels. Throughout her journey, she began to realize she had a calling for ministry. She approached the pastor who replaced my dad at our church and shared her heart with him. A year later, my mom was hired on as the Next Steps Pastor at Crossbridge Community Church. She has the opportunity to walk with individuals in their pain and help them take next steps. I am so proud of her. She uses her story to help bring hope to others.

But the story doesn't end there. After I graduated from Anderson University, Marissa and I moved back to Fort Wayne where I would accept an internship at Crossbridge as the Young Adults Director. For the next seven months, I would be ministering to college students and individuals who are 18-30 years old. On December 5, 2018, I was officially hired as the Young Adults Pastor at Crossbridge Community Church.

Do you see where this story is going?

Even though Crossbridge Community Church lost my dad as the lead pastor, **God declared the story was not over.** God responded to our situation and brought healing to our pain. Five years later, God blessed Crossbridge by doubling the things they had lost. Now, instead of having one Chitwood leading at Crossbridge, there are two—my mom and me. Even though we can't replace everything my dad was able to do, we have the opportunity to use our gifts to bless others. God did not abandon our family or our church. God responded to our pain and blessed us with far more than our former journey. Our pain is still unbearable at times, but God is never letting go of us and will always respond to our circumstances. God does not create our suffering—God is the first responder.

James helped me find healing from God. God is undoubtedly the only place healing will happen. It took me four years to believe that truth, but now that I do, I recognize the power my story can have in helping others.

New Vision

I do not know what your story looks like. I do not know the pain you have experienced. You may have lost a loved one or be battling an illness. You may be financially unstable or without a job. Your family may be dysfunctional or your marriage may be falling apart. Whatever your situation may be, I encourage you to do this: Go to the shack. Go to the place where you once found the most joy but are now avoiding because of the pain it would bring. Invite God to join you at that place and confront Him head on. Wrestle with any questions you may have about life. Shed thousands of tears and scream thousands of words. Allow God to meet you where you are in your pain. It may take one year, five years, or twenty years, but God will always respond to our pain; often in more ways than we even realize. Do not skip the chapters in your life titled Pain, Grief, and Confusion. If you do, you will miss out on the conclusion titled VICTORY. While I was finding reconciliation through my pain, God placed this passage on my heart from Paul's letter to the church in Rome:

> *"Now if we are children, then we are heirs—heirs of God and co-heirs with Christ, if indeed we share in his sufferings in order that we may also share in his glory. I consider that our present sufferings are not worth comparing with the glory that will be revealed in us (Romans 8:17-18, NIV)."*

Other translations say that glory will be revealed to us *later.* I appreciate the NIV the most because it shares that glory is already revealed *in us.* We are experiencing the good that God is creating—even if we do not see it yet.

Your Story

Your story and your brokenness have the power to bring hope to others' stories and brokenness. Your pain can help people find healing in the middle of their pain. Every day we walk by individuals on the streets, in the hallways, throughout our office spaces, and in store aisles, whose lives are filled with *Shattered Windows & Pointless Dreams*. We all have friends or family members in our lives who are experiencing suffering on different levels. What would it look like for us to meet them where they are and use our story to help them recognize that God can provide healing for their pain?

James was that guy for me. James helped me believe God was a good and loving God. He showed me God was big enough to handle all of my sufferings. James helped me realize God was meeting me where I was every single day—because that is how great our God is. Along with James, my wife, my mom, and my siblings were also all-stars for me on this journey. My wife encouraged me and loved me the way I needed to be loved as best she could. Some days that meant silence and other days it meant tears. I have never been the best communicator of my feelings (which I will share in the next chapter), so Marissa has often received the shorter end of the stick in this marriage. However, she rarely complains and is always filled with grace. At the same time, my mom, who lost her husband, is a constant encourager in my life and is always willing to hear my heart and share hers. Along with all of this, my siblings have become my best friends. We have never been closer. My dad would be proud of everything we have accomplished.

Your pain matters, but so does theirs. Use your story to walk with others who are feeling abandoned. It is actually a disservice to God when we hide our stories of healing from others. It is also important that we spend time listening to other people as they share their hearts with us. One of the best ways to do this is to build trust with individuals by listening. I cannot stress enough how damaging the Christian clichés can be when it comes to someone who is suffering....

Just pray more and God will meet you where you are!

Have you gone to church lately?

Have you asked God to take away your pain?

If you truly seek God He will heal you!

While the people who say these things are usually well-meaning, these statements do not provide peace for everyone who is hurting. Many of us have tried doing what these statements suggest over and over again and still feel broken. True healing does not come from saying these clichés, so don't use them. Instead, be real with people. Give individuals a chance to share their hearts and their pain without feeling like you are counseling them. Let those who are hurting swear and scream at God without feeling like you are judging them. Allow individuals a chance to grieve the way they need to. God meets them where they are without expecting perfection and we should too.

The best way to walk with someone in their pain is to show them, not tell them, that God is big enough to handle anything they go through. Be real with everyone. Walk with them in the middle of their pain and their brokenness. Allow God to use you and your story to help others find hope for their pain. Our stories can help change the world. You are never alone in your pain. Even if you feel alone, depressed, stressed, even suicidal, God says there is still a purpose for your life. Let's walk with others and use our stories of God's response in our pain to help them find hope in their pain.

Chapter 9: Shoelaces

"You can give without loving,

but you cannot love without giving." - Amy Carmichael

When is a time you remember falling in love? Now, this love could either be with something or someone. For example, the very first time I tasted my mom's sausage biscuits and gravy, I was hooked. She had the perfect gravy-to-sausage ratio and added some spices that gave it just the right amount of kick. For every single birthday, I would ask my mom to make me sausage biscuits and gravy for dinner so we could end the night with an excellent meal.

I also remember the first time I truly fell in love with *someone*. I have talked about my wife Marissa at various points throughout this book, but I want to share the story of how we started dating and when I fell in love with her so you can understand exactly how awesome she truly is.

Marissa also grew up as a pastor's kid. In fact, her dad and my dad were best friends. While my dad was the lead pastor of Crossbridge Community Church, her dad was the associate and worship pastor. Every holiday, our families would cook out together and play games. I have known Marissa since we were in first grade and thought she was beautiful from the moment I saw her. However, Marissa was funny, smart, beautiful, and mature. I was an awkward middle school boy who was cute, but extremely immature and thought I was hilarious (which meant I wasn't). Oh, and did I mention I was not at all motivated with school? In other words, I had no business pursuing Marissa for a relationship.

In ninth grade, we went on a mission trip to Costa Rica with our church. Both of our dads went on the trip with us, along with twenty other congregants. While we were there, we spent time engaging with the community through sports, music, art, balloon animals, and a lot of laughter. Towards the end of the week, we had a cookout with the church we were partnering with at a campsite. Next to the campsite, there was a river. Marissa and some friends had a great idea that included wading up the river so when we got to the end, we could turn around and float all the way down. Because I was trying to impress her, I did not hesitate to join the team that was going to venture up the river.

As we began the journey, the current was not very strong. While it was challenging, we did not have a difficult time wading through the rocks. All of us were laughing the entire time and could not wait to get to the end of the river so we could turn around and float all the way down.

Uh-Oh

I'm not sure if we came to our senses, or if the water levels decided to rise and the current decided to pick up, but when we turned around and started floating down, it was terrifying. We completely lost control of our bodies and kept banging into trees and rocks. Some of us started going underwater and had a difficult time coming back to the surface. We immediately regretted our decision and were absolutely terrified of the river.

At one point, I was holding onto a tree with my right hand and was able to grab hold of my sister, Taylor, with my left hand. For a few brief seconds, I was the best brother in the world. However, this did not last long.

Out of the corner of my eye, I saw the most beautiful girl floating past me. Like every great brother would do, I let go of my sister Taylor and grabbed Marissa. To this day, Taylor thinks she slipped from my grip.

When I grabbed Marissa, our eyes met, and I was mesmerized. That was the exact moment I fell in love with her. I still have the image locked in my mind today. Six months later we started dating, and then we got married on July 23, 2016. We have been married for three years and have a beautiful Australian Kelpie. Marissa was a rockstar for me when my dad died and has sacrificed so much so I could pursue a life of vocational ministry. She shows me every day what it looks like to love others with grace. I don't deserve her.

As I mentioned in chapter 8, my senior year of college was when I decided to start addressing my grief. Marissa and I got married in our junior year of college, so for an entire year of our marriage, she had to cope with my silence, night terrors, lack of vulnerability, communication issues, depression, and anxiety. There were days when I would come home from work and yell at her for no reason. Instead of abandoning me as any normal person would do, she approached me with love and walked with me through my pain. She continued to encourage me to seek help and prayed for me when I was weakest. That's love, y'all!

During my senior year, James, my counselor, challenged me to be more open with my wife. Our marriage was struggling because of the walls I had placed up in my life. Because of this, James encouraged me to start telling Marissa whenever I was missing my dad. It seems like a small, easy step, but because I had shut out those emotions from my life for the previous four years, there was nothing easy about it. Day after day, I shut down any pain I was feeling and continued to shut out Marissa in the process. Sometimes it was unintentional, but it was always damaging to our relationship and my own emotional state.

I remember sitting on the bed one Tuesday evening after a long day at work. It was 7 p.m. and I was ready to wind down and watch YouTube videos until bed. Unannounced, a huge rush of emotions swept over me. It felt as though a hurricane of pain had collapsed on my chest. Without thinking, I turned over to my wife and said, "I miss my dad..."

And then I lost it. I completely lost it. I broke down crying like a hungry infant. I began weeping and repeating the words, "I miss my dad," and "I want to go home," to Marissa. She began crying with me while she embraced me. In between breaths, Marissa asked me if I wanted to be with my family. I nodded my head yes, and without hesitating, Marissa jumped out of bed and got ready to go. I was such a mess. I could not contain the pain I was experiencing. My grief was overwhelming. I got out of bed, buckled over, and couldn't even stand. I was weeping so uncontrollably that when I went to grab my shoes and put them on, I couldn't. Of course, this made me cry even harder. In the blink of an eye, Marissa dropped what she was doing, grabbed my shoes, put them on me, and started tying my shoelaces. She grabbed my coat, placed it around my shoulders, and then we drove home together crying and listening to some of my dad's sermons.

Just As Christ

Marissa showed me a type of love that night that was nothing short of the love Christ has for each one of us. She met me where I was and tied my shoelaces for me. A grown man couldn't even tie his own shoelaces. I share this story because Christ's love has no boundaries or walls. Jesus healed people society would not touch. Jesus empowered individuals society had given up on. Jesus, holier than anyone, made Himself less than everyone, and loved people no matter what.

I have been asked what I would do if I knew it was my last day to live. Often I say something like spending time with family, eating ice cream all day, and reflecting on memories. Do you know what Jesus chose to do with His last day? Jesus chose to get down on His knees, and wash His disciples' feet. John writes about this in his Gospel.

"It was just before the Passover Festival. Jesus knew that the hour had come for him to leave this world and go to the Father. Having loved his own who were in the world, he loved them to the end. The evening meal was in progress, and the devil had already prompted Judas, the son of Simon Iscariot, to betray Jesus. Jesus knew that the Father had put all things under his power, and that he had come from God and was returning to God; so he got up from the meal, took off his outer clothing, and wrapped a towel around his waist. After that, he poured water into a basin and began to wash his disciples' feet, drying them with the towel that was wrapped around him. He came to Simon Peter, who said to him, 'Lord, are you going to wash my feet?' Jesus replied, 'You do not realize now what I am doing, but later you will understand.' 'No,' said Peter, 'you shall never wash my feet.' Jesus

answered, 'Unless I wash you, you have no part with me.'
'Then, Lord,' Simon Peter replied, 'not just my feet but
my hands and my head as well!' Jesus answered, 'Those
who have had a bath need only to wash their feet; their
whole body is clean. And you are clean, though not every
one of you.' For he knew who was going to betray him,
and that was why he said not everyone was clean. When
he had finished washing their feet, he put on his clothes
and returned to his place. 'Do you understand what I
have done for you?' he asked them. 'You call me
"Teacher" and "Lord," and rightly so, for that is what I
am. Now that I, your Lord and Teacher, have washed your
feet, you also should wash one another's feet. I have set
you an example that you should do as I have done for
you. Very truly I tell you, no servant is greater than his
master, nor is a messenger greater than the one who sent
him. Now that you know these things, you will be blessed
if you do them (John 13:1-17, NIV)."

Jesus, God in the flesh, the disciples' Master and Teacher, got down on His knees and washed His followers' feet. He showed them that regardless of His status He was willing to wash their feet. Now, Jesus says it is our turn. Just as Christ got down on the lowest level to serve the castaways, we must as well.

Just. As. Christ.

We must step through our fear of being uncomfortable and start living like Jesus. Jesus did nothing comfortable. He fasted for forty days and then withstood the devil's temptation to give up His throne (see Luke 4). He went through Samaria instead of around it like every other Jew would do (see John 4). He challenged the Pharisees on their religious views, invited tax collectors to share a meal, and embraced an uncomfortable lifestyle because He knew the weight of this world could only be redeemed by a scandalous love. Marissa gave me a glimpse of God's love that day. In my unbearable grief, she got down on her knees and tied my shoes for me. She was not concerned about how awkward or uncomfortable she may have been. She was only concerned about loving me — just as Christ.

I am beyond grateful for my wife. Marissa is selfless and loving and shows me grace when I need it most. She encourages me to keep going and empowers me to love the least of these. She believes in my dreams and pushes me to move forward. By tying my shoelaces, she showed me what it truly looks like to love people with *Shattered Windows & Pointless Dreams*.

Whether you are single, in a relationship, married, or looking, you can do the same. It may not be the same as my situation, or as intimate, but it can be as powerful. Don't pass by a homeless person without praying for them, and if possible, buying them lunch. Don't go a day without checking in on your friends who are struggling with depression, stress, or anxiety. If your spouse, significant other, or family member is struggling, be for them what Christ is for you: Love. That is going to look different in every situation. For some, it might be tying their shoes; for others it might be talking on the phone, having a date night, or simply hanging out. Don't overthink it. In the simplest ways, Jesus loved everyone—regardless of how shattered their lives were or how pointless society said they were. On the days when I am weakest, Marissa helps me move, and vice versa. Challenge yourself by doing that for your neighbor.

Chapter 10: Privilege Prevails

"Privilege is not in and of itself bad;

what matters is what we do with privilege." - Bell Hooks

A few questions may be running through your mind at this point in the book. Questions such as: "Why me?" or, "What do I have to offer?" or, "Why can't *someone else* pursue others?" or, "What about *me* is so special?"

I wrestled with questions like these for a while. I found myself feeling guilty for thinking this way. I started coming up with excuses for why I could not possibly help or love others. It wasn't until I recognized I was privileged that I started to realize how important it was for me to join the fight.

Privileged.

A word that has many negative connotations.

A word that many are defensive about.

A word that many, including myself at times, deny being...

Privileged.

But here is the truth I recognize: I am one of the most privileged individuals in the world. I am living in the most privileged country, as a white, Christian male, working in the middle class, with a college degree. I have never worried about my next meal. I have never wondered if I was being profiled because of my skin color. I have never been abused because of my gender. I have never been arrested because of my faith. And I certainly have never been *actually* persecuted because I believe in Jesus.

Now, I understand there are definitely numerous exceptions to the rules I stated firmly. If you fit the same description as me and have experienced any or all of the things that I have not, I am sorry. In my experience, the majority of those who fit my description are those who are privileged in the world. Not every time, but certainly most of the time. Luke explains how we should live with our privilege in his Gospel:

> *John answered, "Anyone who has two shirts should share with the one who has none, and anyone who has food should do the same (Luke 3:11, NIV)."*

Privilege is any time we have something beneficial that someone else does not have. This could be a material item or an opportunity. There are individuals who are born into generational poverty who by default, do not have the same privilege as someone born into a middle-class family. Along with this, unfortunately, racism still exists. Denying that our skin color has influence in this world is a lie many still believe. Denying we are living in the most privileged country in the world is also a lie too many of us believe.

Now, is privilege in and of itself a bad thing?

Absolutely not. In fact, it is a great opportunity. Privilege only becomes negative when those of us who are privileged refuse to use our privilege to help others. Privilege only becomes a bad thing when those of us who are privileged refuse to recognize our privilege because of bitterness and entitlement. Often our privilege is something we do not recognize until we are *"woke"* towards those who are underprivileged. We spend our entire lives defensive towards a word, when in fact, it is not a bad thing to be privileged. Being privileged means we have the opportunity and the spiritual obligation to help those in need. Being privileged means we have two shirts to share with those who have none. Being privileged means we can defend the lives of those who are less fortunate and empower those who are marginalized to do amazing things. It is also important that the privileged not just defend those who are marginalized, but place them into position to lead as well—sometimes instead of the privileged.

I woke to my privilege for the first time after I left Fort Wayne, Indiana, to attend school in Chicago, Illinois. My high school was roughly 90% white, Republican, middle/upper class, and Christian. I never had a teacher who wasn't white, and I never saw someone who was living in poverty. I also rarely saw individuals bullied because of their sexuality, religion, or skin color.

All of this changed when I moved to Chicago and started attending North Park University. At North Park, there were numerous demographic differences. The majority of the school was made up of different skin colors than my own. Also, the majority of the students were liberal. Many had different belief systems, including a huge Jewish population right down the road. Language barriers were an issue in Chicago, which made it common for individuals to struggle to communicate while ordering food or getting a haircut. There were thousands of individuals living homeless in the streets of the city. My mind was blown and my heart was broken when I realized how privileged I truly was. One of my best friends from North Park was black. Whenever he and I walked around the city together, there were occasions when he would flinch or put his guard up because of his skin color and the baggage that came with being black. There were times he would not walk up and look at cool expensive cars with me while touristing because he did not want to be profiled. There were times he would get very angry about police shootings—such as the Michael Brown shooting in 2014—that did not impact me the same way. He was constantly living with his radar on, and I rarely understood why... until it hit me. He was marginalized and I was not.

For whatever reason, I was born into the family I was, with the skin color I have, with the money and the college education I do. Some of that was earned and worked for and some of it was given to me. I am not ashamed of these things, and you should not be either. But failure to recognize that there are individuals who are not as fortunate as those of us who have privileges like these is detrimental to the mission of loving God and loving others. Refusing to wake up to the reality that there are underprivileged individuals down the street, needing to be heard and placed in leadership, is claiming Jesus' sacrifice was pointless.

Do not be discouraged if you are living with opportunities others don't have. Do not get defensive towards those who say you are privileged. Instead, we must figure out ways we can use our privilege to empower those who are marginalized. Even if you do not believe your skin color, gender, or economic stability make you privileged, there are clear examples of racism, gender inequality, and poverty still firmly existing today. Refusing to empower those being profiled or judged because of their race, gender, or social status is siding with evil.

Just recently, a white male entered a synagogue in Pittsburgh yelling racial slurs and murdered individuals because of their race and belief system. This presents an opportunity for us white male and female Christians to actively love and support our Jewish brothers and sisters.

I have female friends and family members who are not allowed to teach on stage at church because of male patriarchy. For those of us who believe God empowers women for ministry and leadership roles in the Church (study Deborah, Phoebe, Miriam, Esther, and Priscilla, for just a few of the women leaders in the Bible), it is a man's duty to step aside and surrender our own opportunity to speak and support their vocation.

If you are privileged, do not be offended by your privilege. Instead, use your privilege to defend and empower others. I pray that we recognize God prevails and He will use our privilege to help others prevail. Using our privilege to help those who are less fortunate prevail is exactly what Jesus did. Jesus healed the sick, invited the castaways to share a meal, hung out with sinners, gave a shirt to someone without clothes, fed the hungry, and died on the cross for the least of these. Now it's our turn to use our privilege to help the least, the lost, the lonely, and the forgotten prevail.

Chapter 11: Bleed the Same

"Love everyone today as if today

is the last day of your life." - Debasish Mridha

My fingers whisked away as I pressed down the keys of my laptop one at a time. Statement after statement came out of my mind and onto the screen as I argued on social media. Individuals I had not talked to in years were taking part in the conversation. The conversation at the time was a debate between the phrases "black lives matter," or "all lives matter." Unfortunately, none of us were actually listening to the other side. None of us were taking a step back and viewing the people hidden behind their laptops as humans. None of us were disagreeing with *grace*.

None of us.

I grow weary listening to Christians' arguments and hearing hateful words leave our mouths like a double-edged sword. I grow weary hearing the Church condemn everyone who is a part of the LGBTQ+ community. I grow weary watching

Christians abandon refugees and close the doors to immigrants who are fleeing their oppression. I grow weary watching the media take truths and turn them into lies—or lies and turn them into truths. I grow sick watching people in political and spiritual leadership use their platform to promote immoral use of wealth and riches.

Does anyone else feel this way?

When will we realize beneath our differences, our lifestyles, our choices, our political parties, our faith beliefs, our skin color, our sexual orientation, our sin and our shame, our mistakes and our accomplishments, we all bleed the same? When will we realize we bleed the same as our enemies, the other political party, the other sexual orientation, and our neighbors next door? I have made many mistakes in life, but what I regret most is how I have treated people—in person or online—whom God made in His image.

I must repeat these questions again because they are so vital for understanding the love of Christ: Are we willing to live like *Jesus*? Do we believe God *only pursues us, in America*?

Ouch.

Do we live like we believe God sent Jesus to die for *us*

and not *them?* Because if you still believe this is the case, hopefully this final story will seal the deal for you. Luke paints a perfect example of Jesus' love in his Gospel. He shares a story about Jesus returning to His hometown in Nazareth. The story goes like this:

> *"Jesus returned to Galilee in the power of the Spirit, and news about him spread through the whole countryside. He was teaching in their synagogues, and everyone praised him. He went to Nazareth, where he had been brought up, and on the Sabbath day he went into the synagogue, as was his custom. He stood up to read, and the scroll of the prophet Isaiah was handed to him. Unrolling it, he found the place where it is written: 'The Spirit of the Lord is on me, because he has anointed me to proclaim the good news to the poor. He has sent me to proclaim freedom for the prisoners and recovery of sight for the blind, to set the oppressed free, to proclaim the year of the Lord's favor.' Then he rolled up the scroll, gave it back to the attendant and sat down. The eyes of*

everyone in the synagogue were fastened on him. He began by saying to them, 'Today this scripture is fulfilled in your hearing.' All spoke well of him and were amazed at the gracious words that came from his lips. 'Isn't this Joseph's son?' they asked. Jesus said to them, 'Surely you will quote this proverb to me: "Physician, heal yourself!" And you will tell me, "Do here in your hometown what we have heard that you did in Capernaum." 'Truly I tell you,' he continued, 'no prophet is accepted in his hometown. I assure you that there were many widows in Israel in Elijah's time, when the sky was shut for three and a half years and there was a severe famine throughout the land. Yet Elijah was not sent to any of them, but to a widow in Zarephath in the region of Sidon. And there were many in Israel with leprosy in the time of Elisha the prophet, yet not one of them was cleansed— only Naaman the Syrian.' All the people in the synagogue were furious when they heard this. They got up, drove him out of the town, and took him to the brow of the hill on which the town was built, in order to throw him off the cliff. But he walked right through the crowd and went on his way (Luke 4:14-30, NIV)."

While it may seem like another example of Jesus being rejected, it truly goes so much deeper than a bad breakup story. First, Jesus returns home. After John the Baptist prepares the way and Jesus begins His public ministry, Luke records one of the first things Jesus did was return to Nazareth, the town where He grew up, to teach in the synagogue. It is important to point out that Jesus would have been teaching in front of a Jewish crowd, primarily Jewish leaders (Pharisees). He shares a powerful message about how we are called by the Spirit to proclaim good news to the poor, freedom for the prisoners, sight for the blind, and set the oppressed free.

Good News to the poor.

Freedom for the prisoners.

Sight for the blind.

Set the oppressed free.

The Jewish leaders are ecstatic. They start rejoicing that

their Messiah has finally come. You see, they originally respond with joy because they believe Jesus is saying He is here to proclaim the Good News to *Jews* who are poor, freedom for *Jewish* prisoners, sight for *Jews* who are blind and set oppressed *Jews* free. Per usual, they made it all about *themselves*. However, Jesus came to do something better. Something bigger. Something that not only reaches the Jewish community, but also the Greeks. Something that would include pursuing the Romans and the castaways. Something so powerful it would actually require Jews to take a step back and start pursuing people with *Shattered Windows & Pointless Dreams*.

Just. Like. Jesus.

Clear As Butter

Jesus realizes the Jews in the synagogue are missing the point, and so He uses two stories they can connect with. Jesus takes a Jewish all-star (Elijah) and a Jewish prophet (Elisha) and explains that during their time, they were not strictly sent to heal and help Jewish communities alone. Instead, God sent them to *also* pursue a widow in Zarephath and a leper in Syria—

individuals and communities the Jews despised and neglected. Upon hearing this, the Jewish leaders became angry and attempted to throw Jesus off a cliff. However, Jesus went ghost mode and walked right through the angry crowd towards safety.

I don't think that part of the story gets enough recognition.

Jesus was rejected by His hometown because He challenged His community to not only love people who were their enemies but also view them as His children — *view them as human*. So much so, they would be willing to bring good news to their poor, freedom for their prisoners, sight for their blind, and set their oppressed free. He was rejected for this mindset and later killed for living this way.

And yet, the revolution continued.

Luke wrote in the book of Acts about how Peter and Paul spent their entire ministry attempting to convince Jews and Gentiles that Jesus, God, and the Holy Spirit were for others. While Peter and Paul weren't always perfect in their ministries and sometimes failed at including others (see Galatians 2), they went from city to city planting churches and inspiring individuals to view everyone as God's children. Paul's message to the church in Galatia still rings true today:

> *"There is neither Jew nor Gentile, neither slave nor free,*
>
> *nor is there male and female, for you are all one in Christ*
>
> *Jesus (Galatians 3:28, NIV)."*

Musical artists Mandisa, TobyMac, and Kirk Franklin released a song that has influenced the way I view everyone in an amazing way. Maybe you've heard their song: 'Bleed The Same.' The chorus goes like this:

> *"We all bleed the same*
>
> *We're more beautiful when we come together*
>
> *We all bleed the same*
>
> *So tell me why, tell me why*
>
> *We're divided*
>
> *If we're gonna fight, let's fight for each other*
>
> *If we're gonna shout*
>
> *Let love be the cry*
>
> *We all bleed the same*
>
> *So tell me why, tell me why*
>
> *We're divided"*

Does Cousin Joe happen to be a die-hard liberal? He bleeds the same as you. Does your neighbor happen to be an alcoholic? She bleeds the same as you. Your coworker is an atheist? She bleeds the same as you. The student who is gay? He bleeds the same as you. The little girl who has autism? She bleeds the same as you. The person who cut you off in the middle of a roundabout? He bleeds the same as you.

Individuals with *Shattered Windows & Pointless Dreams* bleed the same as those with white picket fences and six-figure bank accounts.

God says all of us are loved by God, regardless of our baggage (see Romans 5:8). In fact, there is not a single person on this planet God isn't chasing after—hoping one day they accept His love.

Viewing people as children of God who are different from you can be as simple as *listening* without attempting to fix their lives. Because I am a problem solver, I struggle with this. I always want to fix things or debate my point until others agree with my views. When we have a *listen-first* attitude, we can start restoring relationships in our lives. This is not to say that we only listen all the time—there are definitely healthy opportunities for us to share our views or to take control—but even in those moments, we need to make sure we have God's plan of loving everyone in mind, not ours.

Whether we want a wall or open borders, whether we follow Jesus or Buddha, whether we are male or female, whether we struggle with drugs or alcohol, we all bleed the same. It's time we loved like that.

Chapter 12: Say Yes to the Blessed

"Before you look for dirt in people, look for treasure." -

Matshona Dhliwayo

So what now? What do we do with all of this? Where do we go from here?

It's easy! And cheesy...

Say YES to the BLESSED! In Matthew's testimonial account of Jesus, he shares one of his most famous sermons, known as the Sermon on the Mount. It is a very powerful message that directs our attention towards saying yes to pursuing the least, the lost, the lonely, and the forgotten. Many actually believe this sermon was not simply a one-and-done sermon for Jesus; rather, it was a collection of sermons Jesus preached multiple times throughout His life. It goes like this:

> *"Seeing the crowds, he went up on the mountain, and when he sat down, his disciples came to him. And he opened his mouth and taught them, saying: "Blessed are*

the poor in spirit, for theirs is the kingdom of heaven. Blessed are those who mourn, for they shall be comforted. Blessed are the meek, for they shall inherit the earth. Blessed are those who hunger and thirst for righteousness, for they shall be satisfied. Blessed are the merciful, for they shall receive mercy. Blessed are the pure in heart, for they shall see God. Blessed are the peacemakers, for they shall be called sons of God. Blessed are those who are persecuted for righteousness' sake, for theirs is the kingdom of heaven. Blessed are you when others revile you and persecute you and utter all kinds of evil against you falsely on my account. Rejoice and be glad, for your reward is great in heaven, for so they persecuted the prophets who were before you (Matthew 5:1-12, ESV)."

We have evolved into a culture that says "no" or "not right now" too often and too casually. We have turned a blind eye towards the sick and the least of these for too long. We have abandoned the hungry and poor in spirit too naturally. We have left those who are mourning to grieve alone, and we have become peace breakers rather than peacemakers. We have abandoned joy in order to pursue comfort.

No. More.

It is time we started saying yes to pursuing and empowering the blessed. It is time we started helping the poor. It is time we started serving those who are mourning. It is time we started pursuing the hungry. It is time we started loving the persecuted. It is time we started combating human trafficking. It is time we started sitting with the abandoned. It is time we started rejoicing in all things—bringing the Kingdom of Heaven down to earth. When we consider those with *Shattered Windows &* *Pointless Dreams* as blessed, Heaven touches down.

It starts with us.

It starts with me.

It starts with you.

Say *yes* to the *blessed*.

This may seem intimidating at first. This entire book may seem intimidating at first. But it truly is necessary that we shift our mindset and adjust our actions towards saying yes to pursuing those with *Shattered Windows & Pointless Dreams*. This can include opening the door for someone in the morning, paying for the person behind you in the drive-through, buying an extra meal and giving it to a homeless person, providing financial stability for a struggling couple, volunteering for agencies that help fight poverty, empowering teens in broken communities to be leaders, going on mission trips to love on those who have less, and everything in between. Be an active participant in healing what breaks God's heart. We may feel called to help a friend in need or challenged to sit with students being bullied during lunch. While the act may seem small, the effects are powerful.

Trust me, the word will begin to spread that there is something different about us. There is something *powerful* about the way we love. There is something *unstoppable* about the things we share—and it is all because of this Jesus guy we follow. Jesus at times told His followers not to share about the miracles He had done—but they couldn't help it. When we are living the way Jesus did, it is *impossible* to stop the revolution His resurrection started.

What are you called to do? Whom are you called to love? What group are you motivated to pursue? When all you see around you is *Shattered Windows & Pointless Dreams*, choose to replace the broken glass with hope and empower individuals in their dreams. Stop waiting for the next person. As Josh Wilson boldly sang:

> *"I refuse to live like I don't care. I refuse to say another empty prayer, oh I refuse to sit around and wait for someone else to do what God has called me to do myself ("I Refuse" by Josh Wilson)."*

Be that person.

Stop waiting for someone *more qualified*. Stop waiting for someone in a *better situation*. Stop waiting for your courage to step up. Stop waiting for a sign from God. God is waiting for *you* to act.

God does not need boring followers. God wants followers who are excited about pursuing the blessed. God wants individuals who are excited about pursuing the castaways. God wants people who are going to view everyone as His children. Get up and do something. No matter how small it may feel, God is going to use it for something big. Do not allow your circumstances to dictate your reach. If you cannot afford to pay for someone else, pray for them. If you cannot afford to financially help a homeless person, talk with them. If you cannot stand debating Uncle Butch during Christmas, listen to him. Show your neighbors there is something different about you—there is something powerful moving through you.

Something unstoppable is happening right now. Be a part of the movement that is changing the world. Be a part of the mission that pursues everyone. Get ready, because it is going to be a messy, exhausting, and uncomfortable process—but so rewarding. Be like the Jesus who loves those with *Shattered Windows & Pointless Dreams*.

Conclusion: Do You Have A Quarter?

"If you want to know what a man's like, take a good look at how he treats his inferiors, not his equals." - Sirius Black, Harry Potter and the Goblet of Fire, by J.K. Rowling

The other day, I was doing my grocery shopping at Aldi. I love Aldi. I love the prices and how shoppers play a role in keeping Aldi functioning at the level they do. For those who are not aware, in order to take a shopping cart from the store, you need a quarter. You place your quarter in the slot and then take the cart. Once you are done shopping, the incentive to put your cart back is to get your quarter back. As small of an incentive as it may seem... it works.

After I finished shopping I started to return my cart. I was stopped by a mother with three kids. I'll never forget this conversation.

She asked me, "Can I have your shopping cart?" To which I responded, "Do you have a quarter?" She gave me a face and replied, "No, I don't." To which I replied, "If you have a dollar, you can go make the change at the register, but sorry, this is my only quarter."

She walked away with her children and I headed to my car. On the drive home, I started thinking about the conversation. Truthfully, I haven't stopped thinking about the conversation. I still feel guilty about how I responded and the decision I made. I wish I could say this was a long time ago, but it wasn't. I wish I could say it was before I started writing this book, but it wasn't.

I messed up. I got hung up over a quarter when someone needed my help. I was more concerned with keeping what was mine, as small as it was, than I was with showing the love of Christ. I don't know what this woman's story was, but I played a part in making it a more challenging day than it needed to be. There hasn't been a day since that I haven't thought about that lady. There hasn't been a day since that I haven't regretted my actions and wished I could go back and offer her my quarter with a smile on my face.

I share this because I know I am not perfect. I know God is still working on me. I know this book is also for me. I know I have to constantly remind myself who Jesus pursues. I know I make mistakes daily. This is a journey I am on myself. Figuring out how to pursue people with *Shattered Windows & Pointless Dreams* is an everyday battle for me. I did not write this book to let you know I have it figured out. I wrote this book to invite you in on the journey. I am calling for individuals who are willing to lay down their needs for the needs of others. I am asking that you join me in pursuing our neighbors.

I don't want to be known as the guy who held onto his quarter. I don't want to be the guy who ignored the invitation to serve others. I want to be the guy who makes Jesus proud. God designed us to pursue community. It is time we started taking that seriously. There are individuals with different windows and dreams desperate for love. Together, we can fix the windows and empower the dreams of the least, the lost, the lonely, and the forgotten.

Acknowledgements:

I am beyond thankful for God and for all of the experiences I have had through Him. God has been by my side every step of the journey, and for that I am forever grateful. I could not have written this book without His guidance. I am also thankful for my beautiful wife. Marissa has been a constant for me every single day. I truly am blessed with the best. I also want to thank my mama for encouraging me during the writing process and helping me find my voice. I'd also like to thank Dr. Majeski and Pastor Todd. Both have mentored me and helped me grow as a person, a follower of Jesus, and a pastor, in more ways than I can count. Without them, this book would not have been written. I want to thank Kim Chitwood (my mom), Austin Hauptstueck, Kelsi Allen, and Annie Oyer for editing this book, and my wonderful sister-in-law, Meri Colbert, for using your artistic gifts to create the book cover. The hours you all put into this book are unimaginable. Thank you for believing in me and helping me create *Shattered Windows & Pointless Dreams*. I also want to thank my dear friend, Lydia Miller, for sharing her story with the world. She truly is living like Jesus. Thank you to all of the individuals who supported me financially and through prayer to make this book become a reality. Lastly, I am thankful for everyone who has purchased and read this book. I pray this book has impacted you and you have grown closer to loving God and loving others. Life's a journey. I am grateful we are on this journey together.

About the Author

Jordan Daniel Chitwood is a Jesus follower with a vision to carry on the revolution that Jesus started. He has a wife named Marissa and an Australian Kelpie named Theo. Jordan is a Young Adults Pastor and a Teaching Pastor at Crossbridge Community Church with a passion to serve the least of these. He likes to read, write, listen to music, play video games, and hang out with friends in his free time. In the midst of his pain, Jordan believes God is with him every single step of the way. One step at a time, God is molding Jordan into the man God created him to be.

Stay Connected:

Website: jordandanielchitwood.com

Facebook: Jordan Daniel Chitwood

Twitter: Jordan_Chitwood

Instagram: jordan_daniel_chitwood

Made in the USA
Lexington, KY
13 December 2019